PENGUIN BUSINESS

Writers on Organizations

D. S. Pugh is Professor of International Management and Director of Research at the Open University School of Management.

D. J. Hickson is Professor of International Management and Organization at the University of Bradford Management Centre, and Editor-in-Chief of the journal *Organization Studies*.

D. S. Pugh and D. J. Hickson

Writers on Organizations

FOURTH EDITION

Penguin Books

To our parents and to
our professional forebears

PENGUIN BOOKS

Published by the Penguin Group
Penguin Books Ltd, 27 Wrights Lane, London W8 5TZ, England
Viking Penguin, a division of Penguin Books USA Inc.
375 Hudson Street, New York, New York 10014, USA
Penguin Books Australia Ltd, Ringwood, Victoria, Australia
Penguin Books Canada Ltd, 2801 John Street, Markham, Ontario, Canada L3R 1B4
Penguin Books (NZ) Ltd, 182–190 Wairau Road, Auckland 10, New Zealand

Penguin Books Ltd, Registered Offices: Harmondsworth, Middlesex, England

First published by Hutchinson 1964
Second edition published in Penguin Books 1971
Third edition 1983
Fourth edition 1989
10 9 8 7 6 5 4

Printed in England by Clays Ltd, St Ives plc
Filmset in 9/11 Monophoto Times

Contents

Introduction to the Fourth Edition

Throughout the twenty-five years since this book first appeared, it has been in gratifyingly continuous demand. With changing organizational issues and with new work making an impact, it is appropriate now to offer a fourth edition, once again completely revised. We have added descriptions of new writers, brought others up to date, and made some rearrangement of the sections.

It is a commonplace of discussion among managers and administrators that all organizations are different. Even so it is important to study these differences and to classify them. Something useful can thus be said about various kinds of organizations, the ways in which they function and the behaviour of members within them. This book describes the contributions that many prominent writers have made to the understanding of organizations and their management.

In presenting these contributions, our aim has remained the same over the years. It is to give a direct introductory exposition of the views of leading authors whose ideas are currently the subject of interest and debate. We conceive of this work as a resource book giving a general overview of the field, and so we have not essayed critical analysis which would be a quite different task. It is our hope that readers will bring their own critical appraisal to each contribution. Even so we are conscious of the very considerable selection and compression which is involved in presenting a writer's work in a few pages. Some distortions must inevitably result. We can only plead the best of intentions in that our hope is to entice the reader to go to the original listed sources in their richness and complexity. A fully revised edition of the companion volume *Organization Theory: Selected Readings* (edited by D. S. Pugh, Third edition, Penguin Books, 1990) presents extracts from the work of many of the writers summarized here.

One of the attractions of this introductory book is that it should be a relatively slim volume. We have therefore had to balance the addition of new writers with the dropping of others. Their contributions, though, continue to form part of the flow of concepts and theories which nurture the field. We have therefore compiled an omnibus edition, which contains the descriptions of all the writers included in all the editions of this book. Entitled *The Gallery of Writers on Organizations*, this illustrated hard back volume will appear in the coming year. This will allow a fuller exploration of the subject.

It is a source of considerable regret to us that our friend, colleague and co-author of many years, C. R. (Bob) Hinings of the University of Alberta, has found that his current commitments preclude his contributing to this revision. Sadly we accept his decision. We should like to thank him very much for his collaboration on this book over the decades, and look forward to continued fruitful joint participation in other work.

At the University of Bradford Management Centre, we should like to thank Gill Sharpley for her usual impeccable secretarial support and Carlos Arruda Oliveira for compiling the index. Our wives, as always, suffered in the cause.

D. S. PUGH
Open University
School of Management
1989

D. J. HICKSON
University of Bradford
Management Centre
1989

1 The Structure of Organizations

The decisive reason for the advance of bureaucratic organization has always been its purely technical superiority over any other form of organization.
MAX WEBER

It may not be impossible to run an effective organization of 5,000 employees non-bureaucratically, but it would be so difficult that no one tries.
THE ASTON GROUP

The danger lies in the tendency to teach the principles of administration as though they were scientific laws, when they are really little more than administrative expedients found to work well in certain circumstances but never tested in any systematic way.
JOAN WOODWARD

The organization and control of bureaucracy can be designed so as to ensure that the consequential effects on behaviour are in accord with the needs of an open democratic society, and can serve to strengthen such a society.
ELLIOTT JAQUES

The visible hand of managerial direction has replaced the invisible hand of market mechanisms in coordinating flows and allocating resources in major modern industries.
ALFRED D. CHANDLER

If Simple Structure and Machine Bureaucracy were yesterday's structures, and Professional Bureaucracy and the Divisionalized Form are today's, then Adhocracy is clearly tomorrow's.
HENRY MINTZBERG

All organizations have to make provision for continuing activities directed towards the achievement of given aims. Regularities in activities such as task allocation, supervision and coordination are developed. Such regularities constitute the organization's structure and the fact that these activities can be arranged in various ways means that organizations can have differing structures. Indeed, in some respects every organization is unique. But many writers have examined a variety of structures to see if any general principles can be extracted. This variety, moreover, may be related to variations in such factors as the objectives of the organization, its size, ownership, geographical location and technology of manufacture, which produce the characteristic differences in structure of a bank, a hospital, a mass production factory or a local government department.

The writers in this section are concerned to identify different forms of organizational structures and to explore their implications. Max Weber presents three different organizational types on the basis of how authority is exercised. He views one of these types – bureaucracy – as the dominant modern form. Derek Pugh and the Aston Group suggest that it is more realistic to talk in terms of dimensions of structures rather than types. Joan Woodward argues that the production technology is the major determinant of the structure of manufacturing firms

Elliott Jaques has examined the psychological nature of the authority relationships in a bureaucratic structure, and Alfred Chandler shows how management structure is affected by company strategy. Henry Mintzberg describes how the elements of an organization's structure interact to achieve the performance necessary.

All the contributors to this section suggest that an appropriate structure is vital to the efficiency of an organization and must be the subject of careful study in its own right.

Max Weber

Max Weber (1864–1920) was born in Germany. He qualified in law and then became a member of the staff of Berlin University. He remained an academic for the rest of his life, having a primary interest in the broad sweep of the historical development of civilizations through studies of the sociology of religion and the sociology of economic life. In his approach to both of these topics he showed a tremendous range in examining the major world religions such as Judaism, Christianity and Buddhism, and in tracing the pattern of economic development from pre-feudal times. These two interests were combined in his classic studies of the impact of Protestant beliefs on the development of capitalism in Western Europe and the USA. Weber had the prodigious output and ponderous style typical of German philosophers, but those of his writings which have been translated into English have established him as a major figure in sociology.

Weber's principal contribution to the study of organizations was his theory of authority structures which led him to characterize organizations in terms of the authority relations within them. This stemmed from a basic concern with why individuals obeyed commands, why people do as they are told. To deal with this problem Weber made a distinction between *power*, the ability to force people to obey, regardless of their resistance, and *authority*, where orders are voluntarily obeyed by those receiving them. Under an authority system, those in the subordinate role see the issuing of directives by those in the superordinate role as legitimate. Weber distinguished between organizational types according to the way in which authority is legitimized. He outlined three pure types which he labelled 'charismatic', 'traditional', and 'rational–legal', each of which is expressed in a particular administrative apparatus or organization. These pure types are distinctions which are useful for analysing organizations, although any real organization may be a combination of them.

The first mode of exercising authority is based on the personal qualities of the leader. Weber used the Greek term *charisma* to mean any quality of individual personality by virtue of which the leader is set apart from ordinary people and treated as endowed with supernatural, superhuman or at least specifically exceptional powers or qualities. This is the position of the prophet, messiah or political leader, whose organization consists of a set of disciples: the disciples have the job of mediating between the leader and the masses. The typical case of this kind is a small-scale revolutionary movement either religious or political in form, but many organizations have had 'charismatic' founders, such as Lord Nuffield (Morris Motors) and Henry Ford. However, as the basis of authority is in the characteristics of one person and commands are based on that person's inspiration, this type of organization has a built-in instability. The question of succession always arises when the leader dies and the authority has to be passed on. Typically, in political and religious organizations the movement splits with the various disciples claiming to be the 'true' heirs to the charismatic leader. Thus the process is usually one of fission. The tendencies towards this kind of breakdown can be seen in the jockeying for position of Hitler's lieutenants, Himmler and Goering, during the first few months of 1945. It exemplifies the problem of an heir to the leader, and even if the leader nominates a successor, that person will not necessarily be accepted. It is unlikely that another charismatic leader will be present, and so the organization must lose its charismatic form, becoming one of the two remaining types. If the succession becomes hereditary, the organization becomes traditional in form; if the succession is determined by rules a bureaucratic organization develops.

The bases of order and authority in *traditional* organizations are precedent and usage. The rights and expectations of various groups are established in terms of taking what has always happened as sacred; the great arbiter in such a system is custom. Leaders in such a system have authority by virtue of the status that they have inherited, and the extent of their authority is fixed by custom. When charisma is traditionalized by making its transmission hereditary, it becomes part of the role of the leader rather than being part of the founder's personality. The actual organizational form under a traditional authority system can take one of two patterns. There is the *patrimonial form* where officials are personal servants, dependent on the leader for remuneration. Under the *feudal* form the officials have much more autonomy with their own sources of income and a traditional relationship of loyalty towards the leader. The feudal system has a material basis of tithes, fiefs and beneficiaries all resting on past usage and a system of customary rights and duties. Although Weber's examples are historical his insight is equally applicable to modern organizations. Managerial positions are often handed down from one generation to the next as firms establish their own dynasties based on hereditary transmission. Selection and appointment may be based on kinship rather than expertise. Similarly, ways of doing things in many organizations are justified in terms of always having been done that way *as a reason in itself*, rather than on the basis of a rational analysis.

The concept of rational analysis leads to Weber's third type of authority system, the rational–legal one, with its bureaucratic organizational form. This Weber sees as the dominant institution of modern society. The system is called rational because the means are expressly designed to achieve certain specific goals (i.e. the organization is like a well-designed machine with a certain function to perform, and every part of the machine contributes to the attainment of maximum performance of that function). It is legal because authority is exercised by means of a system of rules and procedures through the office which an individual occupies at a particular time. For such organization Weber uses the name 'bureaucracy'. In common usage, bureaucracy is synonymous with inefficiency, an emphasis on red tape, and excessive writing and recording. Specifically, it is identified with inefficient public administration. But in terms of his own definition Weber states that a bureaucratic organization is technically the most efficient form of organization possible. 'Precision, speed, unambiguity, knowledge of files, continuity, discretion, unity, strict subordination, reduction of friction and of material and personal costs – these are raised to the optimum point in the strictly bureaucratic administration.' Weber himself uses the machine analogy when he says that the bureaucracy is like a modern machine, while other organizational forms are like non-mechanical methods of production.

The reason for the efficiency of the bureaucracy lies in its organizational form. As the means used are those which will best achieve the stated ends, it is unencumbered by the personal whims of the leader or by traditional procedures which are no longer applicable. This is because bureaucracies represent the final stage in depersonalization. In such organizations there is a series of officials, whose roles are circumscribed by written definitions of their authority. These offices are arranged in a hierarchy, each successive step embracing all those beneath it. There is a set of rules and procedures within which every possible contingency is theoretically provided for. There is a 'bureau' for the safe keeping of all written records and files, it being an important part of the rationality of the system that information is written down. A clear separation is made between personal and business affairs, bolstered by a contractual method of appointment in terms of technical qualifications for office. In such an organization authority is based in the office and commands are obeyed because the rules state that it is within the competence of a particular office to issue such commands. Also important is the stress on the appointment of experts. One of the signs of a developing bureaucracy is the growth of professional managers and an increase in the number of specialist experts with their own departments.

For Weber this adds up to a highly efficient system of coordination and control. The rationality of the organization shows in its ability to 'calculate' the consequences of its action. Because of the hierarchy of authority and the system of rules, control of the actions of individuals in the organization is assured; this is the depersonalization. Because of the employment of experts who have their specific areas of responsibility and the use of files, there is an amalgamation of the best available knowledge and a record of past behaviour of the organization. This enables predictions to be made about future events. The organization has rationality: 'the methodical attainment of a definitely given and practical end by means of an increasingly precise calculation of means'.

This is where the link between Weber's interest in religion and organizations occurs. Capitalism as an economic system is based on the rational long-term calculation of economic gain. Initially for this to happen, as well as the expansion of world markets, a particular moral outlook is needed. Weber saw this as being supplied by the Protestant religion after the Reformation with its emphasis on this world and the need for individuals to show their salvation through their industry on earth. Thus, economic activity gradually became labelled as a positive good rather than as a negative evil. Capitalism was launched on its path, and this path was cleared most easily through the organizational form of bureaucracy which supplied the apparatus for putting economic rationality into practice. Providing as it does efficiency and regularity, bureaucratic administration is a necessity for any long-term economic calculation. So with increasing industrialization, bureaucracy becomes the dominant method of organizing, and so potent is it that it becomes characteristic of other areas of society such as education, government, politics, etc. Finally, the bureaucratic organization becomes typical of all the institutions of modern society.

Most studies of the formal, structural characteristics of organizations over the past three decades have started from the work of Max Weber. His importance lies in having made the first attempt to produce systematic categories for organizational analysis.

BIBLIOGRAPHY

WEBER, M., *The Protestant Ethic and the Spirit of Capitalism*, Allen & Unwin, 1930.

WEBER, M., *The Theory of Social and Economic Organization*, Free Press, 1947.

GERTH, H. H., and MILLS, C. W. (eds.), *From Max Weber: Essays in Sociology*, Routledge & Kegan Paul, 1948.

Derek Pugh and the Aston Group

In the 1950s, Derek Pugh, now Professor of International Management and Director of Research at the Open University School of Management, UK, brought to the Birmingham College of Advanced Technology (which became the University of Aston-in-Birmingham) a distinctive view of how to conduct research. His research experience as a social psychologist at the University of Edinburgh had placed him in close contact with researchers in other social sciences. He believed that the scope of empirical investigation and of understanding could be widened by multidisciplinary research, founded on a common commitment to and ownership of results within the research team, and on team management skills.

The Industrial Administration Research Unit at Aston led by Pugh between 1961 and 1970 included several 'generations' of researchers whose academic origins ranged from psychology, sociology, economics and politics, to no specific discipline at all. The names which appear most frequently on publications are John Child, David Hickson, Bob Hinings, Roy Payne, Diana Pheysey, and Charles McMillan as the initiator with David Hickson of much subsequent international research, but there are many more. It is symptomatic of the nature of the group that it has not taken on the name of any one individual, even that of Derek Pugh, but it is usually known as the Aston Group, even though there is no longer any special link with that University. The programme of research dispersed with the members of the group, and they and others in touch with them have pursued its work elsewhere in Britain and in several other countries.

The Aston Programme contributed to organization theory by blending some of the research methods and assumptions of psychology with conceptions of organizations and their workings from sociology and economics. Its approach has three essential elements. First, because organizations and their members are changing and complex, numbers of their *attributes should be studied together and as matters of degree*, not as 'either/or' phenomena – a multi-variate approach to a changing world of greys, rather than blacks and whites. This also implies that there will be no single reason for the way in which an organization is set up and run, but many possible influences (i.e. multi-variate causal explanation).

What happens cannot be due to an organization's size alone, nor for that matter to its technology alone, but must in some degree be due to a number of these and other factors all acting together.

Second, because organizations outlast the comings and goings of individuals, it is *appropriate to study their non-personal or institutional aspects* using information on their divisions of work, their control systems and their formal hierarchies. For this, individuals can be interviewed as informants who describe these aspects, rather than being asked to indicate how they experience the organization personally, which they would be if asked to respond to questionnaires about themselves.

Third, because organizations are working wholes, they and their members *should be seen from more than one perspective* to give the fullest possible view. 'The response to the recurring conundrum "does man make organization or does organization make man?" must be to assume that both are happening all the time.' Therefore, the Aston Programme aimed to link:

1. Organizational structure and functioning
2. Group composition and interaction
3. Individual personality and behaviour

Early ambitions to include features of the surrounding society were not realized initially, but began to be included later, when research extended beyond Britain to organizations in other societies.

The Programme commenced with a project in the Birmingham area in England, from which has grown all further research. It focused on the organizational level by studying a highly diverse sample of forty-six organizations: private sector and public sector, from manufacturers of cars and chocolate bars to municipal departments, public services and chain stores. Their formal structures were analysed in terms of their degrees of:

Specialization of functions and roles;
Standardization of procedures;
Formalization of documentation;
Centralization of authority;
Configuration of role structure.

These concepts reflect prevalent ideas about bureaucratization and how to manage, which can be found in the work of Weber (p. 5) and Fayol (p. 85).

A very large number of ways of measuring these aspects of structure were devised which have been employed variously by many researchers since. The most distinctive kind of measure used, an innovation in research on organizations, was based on demonstrating that, for example, the number of functions (such as finance or public relations) that an organization had specialized out of possible specialisms could validly be added to give it a specialization score, and similarly with standardization, formalization, and centralization. This enabled one organization to be compared with another in these terms for the first time.

Despite the range and ramifications of this research, its salient results took on a relatively simple outline. First, the measures of specialization, standardization and formalization were simplified into a combined score for each organization. To distinguish this from its three constituents, it was called *structuring of activities*. An organization with highly structured activities has many specialized sections such as buying, training, work study and so on, and many routine procedures and formal documents, the total effect being that what has to be done is marked out or structured. Second, centralization of decision-making and the autonomy of an organization's decision making from any owning organization were together termed *concentration of authority*. An organization with concentrated authority not only has most of its decisions taken at the top of its own hierarchy but has many decisions taken for it, over its head, by the management of another organization of which it is a wholly or partly owned subsidiary or subordinate section.

Thus at its simplest, the Aston Group isolated two primary elements of any organization, how far the activities of its personnel are structured and how far its decision-making authority is concentrated at the top, which between them sum up much of what an organization is like. Know them and you know it, to a large extent, for they are its two fundamentals.

Although the Aston Programme's approach assumes that organizations are what they are for many reasons, these first results were also relatively simple in the principal explanations that they suggested. A series of features including an organization's purpose, ownership, technology, size and dependence were examined for any correlation with how far an organization had structured its activities or concentrated its authority. It was found that ownership (whether private or public, dispersed in thousands of shareholdings or in the hands of a family) made little difference to structuring and concentration; as did technology, which was reflected in only a few aspects of structure (this qualified and limited the import of Woodward's work (p. 16)).

What did and does matter much more for the form taken by an organization is its *size*, and its degree of *dependence upon other organizations*. The larger it is the more likely its employees are to work in very specialized functions, following standardized procedures and formalized documentation; that is, it will score highly on structuring of activities and have many of the appearances of bureaucracy. The more it is dependent upon only a few owning, supplier, or customer units, or even just one – total dependence is where an organization is wholly owned by another which supplies all its needs and takes all its outputs – the less autonomy it will have in its own decision making, and even those decisions that are left to it are likely to be centralized within itself rather than decentralized.

Yet these results, substantially supported in many later projects, did not mean a working world immovably fixed by a few major elements. Not only did all of these elements change all the time – for organizations grow in size and abolish some formalized documents and introduce others – but all these and the other elements studied were open to *strategic choice*, a concept given prominence by Child in particular. Indeed, these elements had all in some sense been chosen, and were continually being chosen. Managers and administrators choose whether or not an organization is to grow or to enter into contracts that make it dependent upon others. They choose the means of management and control which structure its activities and concentrate its authority. But *one choice constrains another* – each choice (e.g. of size) constrains the options open for the next (e.g. of the degree of structuring to be adopted). A major instance of this is that the choice of how far to develop either of the two primary elements, structuring and concentration, is likely to limit to some extent what can be done with the other, for there is a small negative relationship between them; that is, more of one probably means somewhat less of the other, and to that extent they are alternative means of controlling an organization – not mutually exclusive alternatives (since all organizations use both) but alternative emphases.

Since the first Birmingham area project, the Aston Programme's research in Britain has moved from the original sample of numerous kinds of organization to samples of one kind only such as business firms, trade unions, local governments, and churches, to investigate their particular characteristics. It has extended to many nations worldwide, including the United States and Canada, Western Europe, together with Poland and Sweden, the Middle East and Israel, India, Hong Kong, and Japan. Among the differences which have been found are notably high centralization of organizations under state central planning in Poland, high structuring (specialization and formalization) in Japanese companies which have adopted contemporary Western forms of organization and management, and comparatively less structuring in paternalistic Hong Kong firms. More striking than these differences in the levels of structural characteristics is the consistency in the relationships between these characteristics and size. Analysis by Donaldson, who has been associated with the Aston Group, has shown that in any nation bigger organizations are likely to be more structured but less centralized (though the latter relationship may be weaker in the East). This affirms the *culture-free hypothesis* advanced by Hickson, Hinings, and colleagues that these kinds of basic relationships would hold anywhere irrespective of differences in culture between societies.

Casting their results into an empirically derived taxonomy of forms of organization structure, the Aston Group put forward from their first project a view of the forms prevalent in contemporary industrialized society, in Britain and probably elsewhere too. Large firms, big businesses are typically *workflow bureaucracies*, highly structured but not as highly concentrated in authority as some. Public service organizations of local and central government are *personnel bureaucracies*, not very structured but with highly concentrated authority and procedures focused on hiring, promoting and firing of personnel. Smaller units within large private or public groups are *full bureaucracies*, with the high structuring of the workflow type and the highly concentrated authority of the personnel type. Smaller firms in personal ownership have neither of these features to any great extent, being *non-bureaucracies* (or implicitly structured). There are other types, but these four main ones can be depicted thus:

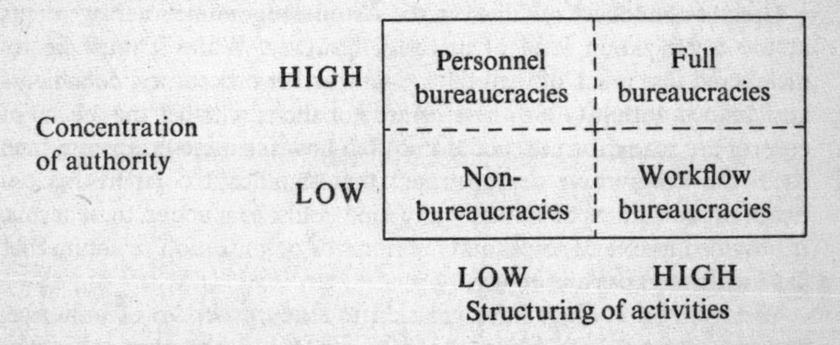

The progression of the Aston Group into research on group and role characteristics and on the individual's experience of organizational 'climate', in accordance with their Programme of linking organizational, group, and individual levels of analysis, is not so well known. Its results are not so clear cut. If any construction can be placed on them overall, it is that they lift from bureaucracy the pall of gloom laid over it by widespread assumptions of its uniformly stifling and dreary nature. It may be like that: but if it is, then it is for those in the lowest-level jobs and not necessarily for those higher in the hierarchy. Life for them differs from one bureaucratic organization to another.

Through a mixture of surveys and of intensive case studies with batteries of methods, Aston researchers showed that while structuring of activities does tend to be associated with greater formality at the group interaction level, and concentration of authority does tend to be associated with less autonomy for individuals and with greater conventional attention to rules, nevertheless a uniformly bureaucratic-type firm can be effective and its personnel can like working in it. At least, this was so in their case study of a small firm owned by a large international corporation, a 'small effective bureaucracy' which they code-named 'Aston'.

In organizations that showed both high structuring and high concentration of authority, which were loosely equated with bureaucracies, there was no evidence of less attractive 'climates' (in terms of the way in which authority was exercised, of interest in work, of routine, and of personal relationships). At the top, such organizations tended to have managers who were younger and better qualified, with more flexible and challenging attitudes. And firms with younger managers tended to show faster growth in sales and assets (though whether youth caused growth or growth attracted younger personnel is an unanswered question). So those managing more bureaucratic-type firms were unlikely themselves to be cautious and conformist, and were more likely to seek innovation and risk.

Greater confidence is shown in the Aston Programme's achievements at the organization level of analysis, however. While it must be remembered that much of their data is on whether procedures, documents and defined authority are there or are not there, whether the means of control are ready for use, and do not tell how far these means are then used, the Programme demonstrated that significant comparisons between organizations of virtually any kind could be made in these terms. It provided usable concepts and measures of organization structure that have withstood use and re-use.

Hickson and Hinings have gone on to study processes of influence, decision-making, and change in organizations. With other colleagues they jointly formulated and tested a 'strategic contingencies theory of intraorganizational power'. This explains why some specialist departments exert more influence in the organization as a whole, while others exert less, by reference to the distinctiveness of their sources of knowledge and skill and how easily they can be replaced.

In an exceptionally wide-ranging study of decision-making, Hickson and colleagues subsequently typified the ways in which strategic decisions are made by top management as *sporadic*, *fluid* or *constricted* and showed that each type had its own distinctive time-scale and behavioural pattern. Hinings (with Greenwood) has traced different tracks followed by organizations as they changed successfully, attempted change unsuccessfully, or remained inert.

BIBLIOGRAPHY

Aston programme books:

PUGH, D. S., and HICKSON, D. J., *Organizational Structure in its Context: The Aston Programme I*, Gower Publishing, 1976.

PUGH, D. S., and HININGS, C. R. (eds.), *Organizational Structure – Extensions and Replications: The Aston Programme II*, Gower Publishing, 1976.

PUGH, D. S., and PAYNE, R. L. (eds.), *Organizational Behaviour in its Context: The Aston Programme III*, Gower Publishing, 1977.

HICKSON, D. J., and MCMILLAN, C. J. (eds.), *Organization and Nation: The Aston Programme IV*, Gower Publishing, 1981.

Aston programme papers:

CHILD, J., 'Organizational Structures, Environment and Performance: the Role of Strategic Choice,' *Sociology* 6 (1972), 2–22.

PUGH, D. S.,'The Measurement of Organization Structures: Does Context Determine Form?' *Organizational Dynamics*, (Spring 1973), 19–34; reprinted in D. S. Pugh (ed.), *Organization Theory*, Penguin, 1990.

DONALDSON, L., 'Size and Bureaucracy in East and West: a Preliminary Meta Analysis,' in S. R. Clegg, D. C. Dunphy and S. G. Redding, *The Enterprise and Management in East Asia*, University of Hong Kong, 1986.

Further work:

HICKSON, D. J., HININGS, C. R., LEE, C. A., SCHNECK, R. E., and PENNINGS, J. M., 'A Strategic Contingencies Theory of Intraorganizational Power,' *Administrative Science Quarterly* 16/2 (1971), 216–29.

HICKSON, D. J., BUTLER, R. J., CRAY, D., MALLORY, G. R., and WILSON, D. C., *Top Decisions*, Blackwell and Jossey-Bass, 1986.

HININGS, C. R., and GREENWOOD, R. G., *The Dynamics of Strategic Change*, Blackwell, 1988.

Joan Woodward

Joan Woodward (1916–1971) was Professor of Industrial Sociology at the Imperial College of Science and Technology, University of London. She began her research career at the University of Liverpool, but she is best known for her subsequent work on technology and organization in manufacturing firms as director of the Human Relations Research Unit at the South-East Essex Technical College. She and her colleagues at Imperial College broadened and deepened this line of research.

From 1953 to 1957 Woodward led the South-East Essex research team in a survey of manufacturing organizations in that area (see Woodward, 1958, 1965). In all, a hundred firms participated; though the amount of information obtained on them varied from firm to firm, and the published information is therefore on smaller numbers. Firms ranged in size from a hundred employees to over a thousand, and some were the main establishments of their companies while others were branch factories. The survey was supplemented by intensive studies of selected firms.

Woodward does not use sweeping classifications of organizations by types (such as those suggested by Weber – charismatic, traditionalistic, bureaucratic – or by Burns – organismic, mechanistic). Rather than attempt in this way to summate whole ranges of characteristics of organizations, she investigates specific features such as the number of levels of authority between top and bottom, the span of control or average number of subordinates per supervisor, the clarity or otherwise with which duties are defined, the amount of written communication, and the extent of division of functions among specialists.

Woodward finds that firms show considerable differences in features such as these. Foremen may have to supervise anything from a handful to eighty or ninety workers; the number of levels of management in production departments may be anywhere from two to eight; communication can be almost entirely verbal or largely written. Why should these differences occur?

Woodward's team compared firms of different sizes, and examined differences in historical background, without finding any answer. But when differences in technology were studied, relationships were seen with many organizational features. It is not claimed as a result that technology is the only influence upon a firm's organization nor that individual managers make no impression, but technology is a major factor.

Woodward finds that the objectives of a firm – what it wishes to make, and for what markets – determine the kind of technology it uses. For example, a firm building novel prototypes of electronic equipment could not do so by the techniques of mass production which dominate vehicle manufacture. Production systems differ in their degree of technical complexity, from unit (jobbing) and small batch production, through large batch and mass production to the most complex, namely process production.

These three broad categories are sub-divided into nine sub-categories of production systems (see Woodward, 1958 for an earlier slightly different version) from least to most complex:

Unit and small batch

1. Production of units to customers' requirements.
2. Production of prototypes.
3. Fabrication of large equipment in stages.
4. Production of small batches to customers' orders.

Large batch and mass production

5. Production of large batches.
6. Production of large batches on assembly lines.
7. Mass production.

Process production

8. Intermittent production of chemicals in multi-purpose plant.
9. Continuous flow production of liquids, gases and crystalline substances.

Some firms used more than one of these production systems and so were placed in additional 'combined system' categories. A distinguishing feature of process systems is that they manufacture products measured by dimensions of weight or volume (e.g. liquids) rather than those usually counted as series of integral units (e.g. numbers of vehicles or of packaged goods).

In general, the higher the category the more it is possible to exercise control over the manufacturing operations because performance can be pre-determined. In a continuous-flow plant such as a chemical installation the equipment can be set for a given result; capacity and breakdown probabilities are known. But in batch production full capacity may not be known and even well-developed production control procedures represent a continual attempt to set fresh targets in the face of many uncertainties of day-to-day manufacture. In unit production of prototypes, for example, it is almost impossible to predict the results of development work.

These differences in technology account for many differences in organization structure. In process technologies where equipment does the job, taller hierarchies are found with longer lines of command, but managed through committees rather than by instruction down the line. Such hierarchies include more trained university graduates; and since the proportion of personnel working directly on production is low, the hierarchy of administrative and managerial personnel is a comparatively large proportion of total employees.

Despite the complex administrative hierarchy of specialist staff and control departments common in large batch and mass production technologies, these have shorter lines of command and proportionately fewer managers and clerks. Their salient characteristic is large numbers of direct production operatives.

Unit and small batch production typically has an even shorter hierarchy where no manager is very far from the production work itself. This relies relatively heavily upon the production personnel themselves without extensive administrative controls.

Some organization characteristics do not differ straight along the nine technology categories. On some, large batch and mass production is often distinctive while unit and process production have much in common with each other. The large numbers of semi-skilled workers on which mass production is based mean that the span of control of supervisors is very wide, and since results are obtained through the pressure exerted by bosses upon subordinates, human and industrial relations may be strained. Typical of both unit and process production are comparatively small groups of skilled workers with more personal relationships with their supervisors.

Similarly, the complex production control problems of large batch and mass systems are reflected in their numbers of staff specialists, greater paperwork, and attempted clear-cut definition of duties, leading to more mechanistic organizations as Burns (p. 41) has called them.

A rough assessment of the firms on both financial and market performance and on reputation showed that the apparently more successful firms had organizational characteristics near the median or average for their category of technology. Perhaps there is one form of organization most appropriate to each system of production. Successful process firms must have taller, more narrowly based, organization pyramids; successful unit production firms must have relatively short pyramids; and so on.

Certainly more prolonged case-studies carried out by Woodward and her colleagues to test out the results of the initial survey showed that a change of technology category seems to force changes in organization. This in itself may bring conflict among those whose interests are affected, especially if the change is into batch type production. Firms were studied which moved from unit to batch, attempts being made to rationalize and increase the scale of production; and from process to batch, where for example a firm began to package a product previously sold in bulk. In such cases, middle managers and supervisors find that in batch production their days disappear in a confusion of calls and contacts with other people, that this subjects them to greater personal stress, and that their responsibility for production overlaps with that of new planning and control departments.

Indeed, such changes in technology may alter the whole status of the several functions in a firm. This is because the cycle of manufacture places development, production and marketing in a different order in different technologies. In unit or jobbing systems, marketing precedes development and production follows last, since not until a customer requires a product and it is designed can production occur. In large batch and mass systems, the development and production of a new line precedes its mass marketing. In process systems, development of a possible product and marketing to assured customers must precede commitment of capital to special purpose plant to produce it. In each system, the most critical function is the central one which has the greatest effect on success. That is, in unit systems, development has most importance and status; in mass systems it is production; in process systems it is marketing.

Woodward and her colleagues have carried out further detailed case studies of managerial control in its various forms as the link between the technology of manufacture and organizational structure and behaviour. In *Industrial Organization: Behaviour and Control*, Reeves and Woodward focus upon two dimensions of managerial control systems: first, the extent to which control varies between being personal and impersonal; secondly, the degree to which control is fragmented.

Along the first dimension, there is a range of control systems from completely personal hierarchical control at one extreme, as operated by an owner-employer, to completely impersonal mechanical control at the other, as operated by measurement mechanisms and the automatic controls of machine tools. In the middle of the range come the impersonal control processes which are based on administrative procedures, such as production planning and cost systems. Firms may be compared along this dimension, which is associated with characteristic effects upon structure and behaviour. The most important effect is that movement towards impersonal control involves a separation between the planning and execution stages of the work process.

At the personal end of the scale there is almost total overlap between planning and execution; with impersonal administrative control processes there is considerable separation but the planning departments such as production control, quality control and cost control are involved in the execution of the work; at the mechanical end of the scale there can be total separation – the control designers and planners not being concerned at all with the operations since they have already built in correction mechanisms at the planning stage. Indeed the planning and design stages at the mechanical control end of the scale may be the concern of a separate organization, as when a chemical engineering firm undertakes the design and erection of an automated continuous-flow chemical plant complete with mechanical control processes, which is then handed over to the contracting organization.

The second dimension of control systems studied by Reeves and Woodward was the extent to which control was fragmented, ranging from a single integrated system of control at one extreme, to multi-system fragmented control at the other. To obtain a single integrated system, a firm would continuously attempt to relate the standards set for various departments to the performance and adjustment mechanisms associated with them. At the other end of the scale, a firm might have a number of control criteria operating independently which are continuously reconciled by the supervisor or the production operative. A job has to be done by a particular date as set by production control, to a particular standard as set by quality control, to a cost limit as set by cost control, by particular methods as set by work study, and so on. An inevitable result of having a multiplicity of systems with fragmented control is conflict, when supervisors attempt to satisfy each of the control criteria and in doing so jeopardize their performance on the others.

The two dimensions of control processes are used together to generate a four-fold typology of systems in a developmental sequence. Four categories are outlined:

1. Firms with unitary and mainly personal controls, such as an entrepreneurial firm, where the owner would personally relate time and quality to cost. This type is characteristic of unit and small batch production.
2. Firms with fragmented and mainly personal controls, such as a firm where more individuals were involved in setting control criteria.
3. Firms with fragmented and mainly impersonal administrative or mechanical controls, such as a firm where the control criteria are

impersonally set by functional departments. Most large batch and mass production firms fall here or in category 2.

4. Firms with unitary and mainly impersonal administrative or mechanical controls, such as a firm controlling the total manufacturing process to a master plan, perhaps using a computer for information processing and process control. This type is characteristic of process production.

The basic assumption and conclusion of Woodward's work is that meaningful explanations of differences in organization and behaviour can be found in the work situation itself. The technology of this work situation should be a critical consideration in management practice. There is no one best way. She warns against accepting principles of administration as universally applicable. The same principles can produce different results in different circumstances; many principles derive from experience of large batch or mass production only and are not likely to apply in other technologies. Careful study of the objectives and technology of a firm is required.

Woodward's study pioneered both in empirical investigation and in setting a fresh framework of thought. Prior to it, thinking about organization depended on the apt but often over-generalized statements of experienced managers, and on isolated case-studies of particular firms. Woodward showed the possibilities of comparisons of large numbers of firms so that generalizations might be securely based and their limits seen.

She forces thinking away from the abstract elaboration of principles of administration to an examination of the constraints placed on organization structure and management practice by differing technologies and their associated control systems.

BIBLIOGRAPHY

WOODWARD, J., *The Dock Worker*, Liverpool University Press, 1955.

WOODWARD, J., 'Management and technology', *Problems of Progress in Industry* 3, HMSO, 1958.

WOODWARD, J., *The Saleswoman: A Study of Attitudes and Behaviour in Retail Distribution*, Pitman, 1960.

WOODWARD, J., *Industrial Organization: Theory and Practice*, Oxford University Press, 1965, 2nd edn 1980.

WOODWARD, J. (ed.), *Industrial Organization: Behaviour and Control*, Oxford University Press, 1970.

Elliott Jaques and the Glacier Investigations

Elliott Jaques is a Canadian who graduated in psychology at the University of Toronto and later in medicine at the Johns Hopkins Medical School. After service in the Royal Canadian Army Medical Corps, he joined the staff of the Tavistock Institute of Human Relations, where over a period of years he led a study of worker and management activities in the Glacier Metal Company – an engineering factory in London whose managing director was Wilfred Brown, himself a well-known writer on management issues. The Glacier Investigations may well come to bear comparison with the Hawthorne Studies for their impact on management thinking. For this work Jaques was awarded a Doctorate of Philosophy in the Department of Social Relations at Harvard University. He is a qualified Kleinian psychoanalyst and has worked as a psychotherapist and as a 'social therapist' to the Glacier Company. Jaques has been Professor of Social Science and Director of the Institute of Organization and Social Studies at Brunel University and has worked with the National Health Service, the Church of England, and with many commercial and public organizations in Europe and America.

Jaques and his collaborators in the Glacier Investigations use the technique of 'action research'. They work in collaboration with members of the firm to study psychological and social forces affecting group behaviour; to develop more effective ways of resolving social stress; and to facilitate agreed and desired social change.

The problems they tackle are those on which particular groups in the organization request their help. Thus Jaques's book *The Changing Culture of a Factory* describes, for example, studies of problems of payment and morale in the Service Department, worker–management cooperation in the Works Committee, executive leadership at the Divisional Managers' meeting. The method used consists of the 'working-through' (by the investigator and the group together) of current problems and their possible solutions. The investigator attends meetings of the group, and interprets to it the social and personal factors at play in an attempt to increase the social and psychological insight of the group. This also promotes a more rational attitude to social change.

The 'working-through' process usually leads to the discovery that the apparent problems of the group are only symptoms of more basic and long-term difficulties and these are then examined. What began as an issue of wages and methods of payment in the Service Department, for example, soon developed into the complex ramifications of inter-group stresses so often associated with wage questions. As a result of the working-through of management and worker differences at a series of meetings of representatives of both sides (which was facilitated by the investigator's intepretations), not only was the change-over to a new system of payment accomplished, but ın the new situation created by these discussions it was possible to institute a Shop Council as a continuing mechanism through which members could take part in setting policy for the department.

One of the most important findings to come out of the Glacier Investigations is people's felt need to have their role and status clearly defined in a way which is acceptable both to themselves and to their colleagues. Where there is some confusion of role boundaries, or where multiple roles occupied by the same person are not sufficiently distinguished, insecurity and frustration result. The study of the Divisional Managers' meeting showed that it functioned sometimes as an executive management committee taking decisions for the London factory, sometimes as a group for non-decision-making discussions with the Managing Director, and sometimes as a concealed Board of Directors for the whole company (including the Scottish factory). In this mixture of different functions, the same group had different powers over the affairs of the organization, depending on the particular capacity in which it was functioning. But these powers were not clear and this was personally disturbing to the members.

Even when a role has been defined it may contain elements which the individual finds unacceptable or difficult to fill. In an organization committed to consultative management, a superior may become increasingly unwilling to exercise authority. Jaques describes some mechanisms by which responsibility and authority may be avoided. One is the exercise of a consultative relationship only. Thus the Managing Director failed to perceive that he also held a role as chief executive of the London factory, and adopted only a consultative Managing Director's role to the Divisional Managers. This left a gap in the executive hierarchy. Another mechanism is the misuse of the process of formal joint consultation. This often provides an escape route from accepting responsibility for immediate subordinates, by making possible easy and direct contact between higher management and workers' representatives. Thus to make consultative management work, the consultation must follow the chain of command; otherwise conflict arises from those by-passed. Yet another evasive possibility is pseudo-democracy: a superior asserting 'I'm just an ordinary member of this committee' while being in fact the most senior person present; or a superior avoiding the leadership role by excessive delegation. One of the most important conclusions is that there is a distinctive leadership role in groups that members expect to be properly filled; and groups do not function well unless it is.

At the conclusion of these Tavistock studies, Jaques changed his position, becoming, with the consent of the workers' representatives, a part-time employee of the firm. He still retained his independent position, however, and continued his role as 'social analyst', working on problems of wages and salaries. Previous discussion had revealed continuous problems arising from supposed unfair differences in pay, and the task was to determine the appropriate payment and status of individuals. How can one establish what will be generally accepted as the right level of pay for a given job, particularly in relation to other jobs?

Work was divided by Jaques into its prescribed and its discretionary content. Prescribed work is specified in such a way as to leave nothing to the judgement of the individual doing it. But *all* jobs have some content, however small, which requires the individual to use discretion. From this developed the concept of the 'time-span of discretion' – the idea that the main criterion by which the importance of a job is implicitly evaluated is the length of time which expires before decisions taken by an individual are reviewed and evaluated. At the lowest level what the individual does is frequently checked, but at the highest level it might take several years before the effectiveness of a decision shows up. This approach is developed by Jaques in *The Measurement of Responsibility*.

Jaques finds that there is not a continuous increase in range of time-spans of discretion as one goes up the organization – in fact the changes go in steps. He identifies seven major strata (although there are sub-steps within each) up to three months, up to one year, two years, five years, ten years, twenty years, more than twenty years. These are generally recognized as clear differences of level, worthy of differences in payment. Those working in level one accept that those with level two discretion should be paid more and all would feel it inequitable if they were not. Differentials in 'felt-fair pay' – what people think they and others should earn – are very highly correlated (0.9 in the Glacier Metal Company) with objective measurements of differences in time-span, so that if a payment system is based on the discretion differences between jobs it will generally be seen as equitable.

A third element is the growth in capacity of the individual to operate with greater discretion, and Jacques presents earning progression curves which identify appropriate payments for those capable of, and on their way to, higher levels of discretion. Individuals function best when working at a level which corresponds to their capacity and for which they obtain equitable payment, and appropriate opportunity must be given for individuals to progress to their maximum time-span capacity.

These arguments are developed in *Free Enterprise, Fair Employment* to reject both Keynesian and monetarist economic measures as inadequate for dealing with self-perpetuating inflationary movements which then cause unemployment. Jacques argues that any nation has as much work as it wants for everyone, regardless of economic conditions. But there is one prime condition for full employment without inflation: the achievement of equitable pay differentials by political consensus based on the equitable work payment-scale appropriate to different time-span levels. Jacques presents evidence that in 1980, for example, the equitable annual wage and salary levels for a time-span of discretion of three months was £7,000 in England and $20,500 in the U S, whereas for a two year time-span job it was £19,500 and $60,000. (The actual monetary levels will, of course, change over the years depending upon the rate of earnings inflation.)

The figures are not for the *actual* levels of pay in 1980 but for what people felt was differentially fair at that time. Any systematic policy for wages and salaries must decide (i) what the general level should be this year compared with last year, and (ii) whether any adjustment of differentials is called for – should the rates for the time-span levels be compressed, or expanded, in the whole of the range or part of the range, etc. These are the issues for a rational policy and Jacques maintains they would be accepted as just and fair as long as the differences in time-span of discretion were objectively determined and recognized.

Levels of time-span of discretion and the individual's work capacity to operate in these are also the keys to Jaques's general theory of bureaucracy. A bureaucracy in Jaques's terms is a hierarchically stratified employment system in which employees are accountable to their bosses for work that they do. This particular definition (which is somewhat different from the usual one – see Weber, p. 5) means that, for example, universities which have collegiate accountability of academic staff, or trade unions which have electoral accountability of full-time officers, are not bureaucracies in this sense. Jaques is insistent that neither his theory of bureaucracy nor his theories of time-span of discretion and equitable payment are intended to apply in such organizations.

In bureaucracies (such as business firms, government agencies, armed services) Jaques has found that ascending the hierarchy involves operating with increasing time-spans and that the basic seven strata of time-span correspond with levels of thinking capability from concrete thinking at the bottom end to abstract modelling and institution-creating at the top. The capacity to operate at longer time-spans with higher levels of abstraction in reasoning is the determinant of effectiveness at the higher levels of bureaucracy. The reason why bureaucracies are pyramidal in shape is that this work capacity (which Jaques maintains is innate) is very differentially distributed in human populations. Fewer are capable of the higher abstractions, and this is indeed generally recognized by organization members. It is this consensus which would allow equitable payment based on time-span capacity to operate in economic competition *without* the exploitation of labour.

BIBLIOGRAPHY

JAQUES, E., *The Changing Culture of a Factory*, Tavistock, 1951.
JAQUES, E., *The Measurement of Responsibility*, Tavistock, 1956.
JAQUES, E., *Equitable Payment*, Heinemann, 1961; Penguin, 1967.
JAQUES, E., *A General Theory of Bureaucracy*, Heinemann, 1976.
JAQUES, E., *Free Enterprise, Fair Employment*, Heinemann, 1982.
BROWN, W., and JAQUES, E., *Glacier Project Papers*, Heinemann, 1965.

Alfred D. Chandler

Alfred Chandler is Straus Professor of Business History in the Graduate School of Business Administration, Harvard University. He is an economic historian and his research work has centred on the study of business history and, in particular, administration. He has long argued that this is a much neglected area in the study of recent history. His studies of big business have been carried out with grants from a number of sources including the Alfred P. Sloan Foundation. His work has been internationally recognized, and his book *The Visible Hand* was awarded the Pulitzer Prize for History and the Bancroft Prize. Chandler has taught at a variety of universities in the United States and Europe.

All of Chandler's academic work has been concerned with the theme of the rise and role of the large-scale business enterprise during what he describes as the formative years of modern capitalism. These are the years 1850–1920. He suggests, from his many studies, that during this period a new economic institution was created, the multi-unit firm, controlled by a new class of managers operating within a new system of capitalism. These new managers had to develop strategies different from those of their entrepreneurial predecessors and be particularly innovative in creating structures to implement those strategies. The reasons for this shift are to be found in changes in demand bringing about mass markets and technological change which allowed high volume production. The new organization structures allowed the integration of mass production with mass distribution.

While Chandler's analysis is historical, he makes general points about organizational change and the relationship between strategy and structure. In particular, from his studies, Chandler is clear that the structure of an organization follows from the strategy that is adopted. The distinction between these two is crucial. *Strategy* is the determination of basic long-term goals and objectives together with the adoption of courses of action and the allocation of resources for carrying out those goals. *Structure* is the organization which is devised to administer the activities which arise from the strategies adopted. As such it involves the existence of a hierarchy, the distribution of work and lines of authority and communication. In addition, the concept of structure covers the information and data that flow along those lines.

Once an organization moves away from the small, owner-controlled enterprise towards the modern, multi-unit business enterprise then the new class of managers appears. This is important for structural developments because the salaried manager is committed to the long-term stability of the enterprise. The managerial hierarchy gives positions of power and authority and as a result becomes both a source of permanence and continued growth. As part of this process the careers of salaried managers become increasingly technical and professional.

The role of management in developing structure is central to Chandler's analysis. As he puts it, 'the visible hand of management has replaced Adam Smith's invisible hand of market forces'. Managers are both products of, and developers of, the multi-divisional, decentralized structure which is the organizational outcome of technological change and rising demand. They become responsible for the administration of the enterprise, that is, coordinating, planning and appraising work, and allocating resources.

The structural arrangements of a large business enterprise have to allow for both the efficient day-to-day operations of its various units and for dealing with the long-run health of the company. The developments which follow from this involve operating with a decentralized structure to deal with day-to-day manufacturing and services, and building up a central office with functional departments to manage the long-run prospects of the company. This is all part of the process of specialization of functions as a major structural device. The key distinctions are between the general office, divisions, departments and field units. Each of these has a particular function and one of the basic reasons for the success of this type of structure is that it clearly removed from the immediate operations those executives responsible for long-term planning and appraisal. The significance of this separation is that it gives those executives the time, information and psychological commitment for long-term activities.

The introduction of this distinctive organizational structure with its unique managerial hierarchy marked the transition from a family- or finance-based capitalism to managerial capitalism. But because, in Chandler's view, structure follows strategy this transition could only occur in response to external pressures. Particularly important was the increasing volume of activity which arose in response to the new national and increasingly urban markets of the late nineteenth century. Together with this was the technological change which enabled enterprises to move into high-volume production.

In the face of such pressures, enterprises could adopt either defensive or positive strategies. A *positive strategy* occurs when an enterprise actively looks for new markets and new products to serve those markets.

It is organized around product diversification. A *defensive strategy* is where an enterprise acts to protect its current position. The common way of achieving this is to form a vertically integrated company by means of mergers with similar enterprises, suppliers and customers.

Both strategies lead to bigger organizations which have administrative problems. This begins a systematization of techniques for the administration of functional activities. An initial type of organization for achieving this is the centralized, functionally departmentalized structure. It enables the necessary new expert skills to be brought in but retains control by the owners. But the increase in scale of organizations involves building up capacity and enlarging the resources of people, money and materials at the disposal of an enterprise. A result of this is further and continuing growth to ensure the full use of those resources, a result which emanates from the interests of the new managers rather than the owners. Growth becomes internally as well as externally generated and then produces the really innovative structure, that of the multi-unit decentralized form.

To illustrate his points in detail and to chart the process of structural innovation, Chandler looks at the cases of four companies: Du Pont, General Motors, Standard Oil of New Jersey and Sears Roebuck. According to Chandler, the general pressures and needs facing these four companies were the same. Also in general terms, the structural outcome was very similar. But the process of diagnosing the issues and introducing the consequent administrative changes was quite different.

The particular structural innovation of Du Pont was to create autonomous divisions. The company reached the beginning of the twentieth century as a loose federation with no central administrative control. The first strategy of the younger Du Ponts was to centralize control and concentrate manufacturing activity in a few, larger plants. This was the centralized, functionally departmentalized structure. Important to the operation of the company was the development of new forms of management information and forecasting. The introduction of the multi-unit, decentralized structure came with the need to maintain growth. It was done by basing the structure on a new principle, coordinating related effort rather than like things. This innovative principle meant that different broad functional activities had to be placed in separate administrative units. To operate these units, the executives responsible were given enhanced authority. Eventually these developed into product-based units backed by a central, general office to deal with strategic issues. This left the autonomous units to get on with day-to-day operations.

The General Motors case underlines the need for structure to follow strategy. William Durant, the founder of General Motors, went for a volume strategy with many operating units in an extremely loose federation. There was a crisis in 1920 due to lack of overall control. The response of Alfred P. Sloan, who became the Chief Executive Officer in 1923, was to create a general office to be responsible for broad policies and objectives and to coordinate effort. A line-and-staff structure was developed, allowing the product divisions to ensure good use of resources and a proper product flow, with the headquarters staff appraising divisional performance and plans. The new structure took five years to put in place.

Sloan has described in *My Years with General Motors* the nature of the problems and the need for changes as he saw them from the Chief Executive's point of view. Top management has the basic tasks of providing motivation and opportunity for its senior executives; motivation by incentive compensation through stock option plans, and opportunity through decentralized management. But coordination is also required, and good management rests on a reconciliation of centralization and decentralization. It was through his attempts to obtain the correct structural balance between these extremes that Sloan enunciated his seemingly paradoxical principle of 'coordinated decentralization'. His aim was coordinated control of decentralized operations. Policy coordination is achieved through committees. It is evolved in a continuous debate to which all may contribute, and is basically an educational process. Executive administration is the clear responsibility of individuals who carry out the evolving policy.

As with General Motors, Standard Oil of New Jersey was, for Chandler, a case of initial failure to adjust structure to strategy. The channels of authority and communication were insufficiently defined within a partly federated, partly consolidated company. As a result there was a series of crises over inventories and over-production during the 1920s which led to *ad hoc* responses. The initial development was to build up a central office for resource allocation and coordination. A second stage was to set up a decentralized divisional structure. According to Chandler, the response in Standard Oil was slower and more tentative than in Du Pont or General Motors partly because the problems were more difficult and partly because of a general lack of concern with organizational problems.

During the 1920s and 1930s, Sears Roebuck underwent the same process in its own particular way, partly planned and partly unplanned. The initial defensive strategy of vertical integration produced a centralized, functionally departmentalized structure. Continued growth produced the pressure for decentralized, regional organization and for sorting out the relationships between operating units and functional departments. Contributors to the book edited by Chandler and Daems trace similar processes in French, German and British industry.

For Chandler, both his case studies and his broader work illustrate a number of general points about structural development and organizational innovation. The first is that the market and technological pressures of an urban, industrial society push enterprises in the same structural direction, but the actual process of innovation can be quite different. In this process it is important to distinguish between an adaptive response and a creative innovation. An *adaptive response* is a structural change which stays within the range of current custom and practice as was the case with functional departments and a central office. A *creative innovation* goes beyond existing practice and procedures, developing decentralized field units for example. The general adoption of a line-and-staff departmental structure meant that delegation of authority and responsibility to field units was possible.

From this process, says Chandler, there arises a new economic function in society, that of administrative coordination and control. To carry out that function, a new species is created, the salaried manager. In carrying out the function the modern business enterprise is produced, with its two specific characteristics – the existence of many distinct operating units and their management by a hierarchy of salaried executives.

BIBLIOGRAPHY

SLOAN, A. P., *My Years with General Motors*, Sidgwick and Jackson, 1965.

CHANDLER, A. D., *Strategy and Structure*, MIT Press, 1962.

CHANDLER, A. D., *The Visible Hand: The Managerial Revolution in American Business*, Harvard University Press, 1977.

CHANDLER, A. D., and DAEMS, H. (eds.), *Managerial Hierarchies: Comparative Perspectives on the Rise of Modern Industrial Enterprises*, Harvard University Press, 1980.

CHANDLER, A. D., and TEDLOW, R. S., *The Coming of Managerial Capitalism*, Irwin, 1985.

Henry Mintzberg

Henry Mintzberg is Bronfman Professor of Management at McGill University, Montreal. He graduated from the Sloan School of Management at the Massachusetts Institute of Technology. Among a variety of consulting assignments and visiting appointments, he has been visiting professor at the University of Aix-en-Provence in France. He has studied what managers actually do as they manage, and what kinds of organization they are managing.

Mintzberg shows a substantial difference between what managers do and what they are said to do. On the basis of work activity studies he demonstrates that a manager's job is characterized by pace, interruptions, brevity, variety and fragmentation of activities, and a preference for verbal contacts. Managers spend a considerable amount of time in scheduled meetings and in networks of contacts outside meetings.

The fragmentary nature of what managers do leads to the suggestion that they have to perform a wide variety of roles. Mintzberg suggests that there are ten managerial roles which can be grouped into three areas: *interpersonal*, *informational* and *decisional*.

Interpersonal roles cover the relationships that a manager has to have with others. The three roles within this category are figurehead, leader and liaison. Managers have to act as *figureheads* because of their formal authority and symbolic position, representing their organizations. As *leaders*, managers have to bring together the needs of an organization and those of the individuals under their command. The third interpersonal role, that of *liaison*, deals with the horizontal relationships which work-activity studies have shown to be important for a manager. A manager has to maintain a network of relationships outside the organization.

Managers have to collect, disseminate and transmit information and have three corresponding informational roles, namely monitor, disseminator and spokesman. A manager is an important figure in *monitoring* what goes on in the organization, receiving information about both internal and external events, and transmitting it to others. This process of transmission is the *dissemination* role, passing on information of both a factual and value kind. A manager often has to give information concerning the organization to outsiders, taking on the role of *spokesman* to both the general public and those in positions of influence.

As with so many writers about management, Mintzberg regards the most crucial part of managerial activity as that concerned with making decisions. The four roles that he places in this category are based on different classes of decision, namely, entrepreneur, disturbance handler, resource allocator and negotiator. As *entrepreneurs*, managers make decisions about changing what is happening in an organization. They may have to both initiate change and to take an active part in deciding exactly what is to be done. In principle, they are acting voluntarily. This is very different from their role as a *disturbance handler*, where managers have to make decisions which arise from events beyond their control and unpredicted. The ability to react to events as well as to plan activities is an important managerial skill in Mintzberg's eyes.

The *resource allocation* role of a manager is central to much organizational analysis. Clearly a manager has to make decisions about the allocation of money, people, equipment, time and so on. Mintzberg points out that in doing so a manager is actually scheduling time, programming work and authorizing actions. The *negotiation* role is put in the decisional category by Mintzberg because it is 'resource trading in real time'. A manager has to negotiate with others and in the process be able to make decisions about the commitment of organizational resources.

For Mintzberg these ten roles provide a more adequate description of what managers do than any of the various schools of management thought. In these roles it is information that is crucial; the manager is determining the priority of information. Through the interpersonal roles a manager acquires information, and through the decisional roles it is put into use.

The scope for each manager to choose a different blend of roles means that management is not reducible to a set of scientific statements and programmes. Management is essentially an art and it is necessary for managers to try and learn continuously about their own situations. Self-study is vital. At the moment there is no solid basis for teaching a theory of managing. According to Mintzberg 'the management school has been more effective at training technocrats to deal with structured problems than managers to deal with unstructured ones'.

Nor has management teaching given the practitioner a ready way of understanding the design of organizations. Mintzberg sets out to devise such a way. As he sees it, there are five basic designs whose features recur in published research. He calls them the Simple Structure, the Machine Bureaucracy, the Professional Bureaucracy, the Divisionalized Form, and the Adhocracy.

The primary feature which distinguishes each from the others is that within each, one from among five basic parts of organization predominates (it is the repetition of the number five that prompts Mintzberg to call his 1983 book, *Structure in Fives*). In a Simple Structure, the key part that predominates is the 'strategic apex', which in a manufacturer, for example, would be the Board of Directors, President or Chief Executive, and their personal staff. In a Machine Bureaucracy, it is the 'technostructure', which would include the personnel in planning, finance, training, operations research and work study, and production scheduling. The key part in a Professional Bureaucracy is the 'operating core', those at the working base of the organization. While in a manufacturer this would be the buyers, machine operators, salespeople, and despatchers, in a Professional Bureaucracy it might be doctors and nurses (in a hospital) or teaching staff (in a college). The 'middle line' are key in the Divisionalized Form of organization, being the personnel who 'manage managers' in the hierarchy between the strategic apex and the operating core. In manufacturing these would include the heads of the production and sales functions, and the managers and supervisors beneath them. Finally, in an Adhocracy the 'support staff' are the key part. In a typical manufacturer they might be in public relations, industrial relations, pricing, payroll, even the cafeteria, as well as in research and development, but in an Adhocracy the focus is upon the latter, the 'R & D'.

Each of the five parts exerts a 'pull' upon the organization. 'To the extent that conditions favour one over the others, the organization is drawn to structure itself as one of the configurations', or designs. It is pulled towards one more than towards the others.

The first, the *Simple Structure*, in which the strongest pull is by the *strategic apex* towards centralization, is as simple as its name indicates. It has little or no technostructure, few support staff, minimal differentiation between departments, and a small hierarchy. Coordination is by direct supervision, downwards from the strong apex where power is in the hands of the chief executive: so it does not need formal planning or training or similar procedures, and can be flexible and 'organic' (see also Burns, p. 41). The conditions favouring this Simple Structure are those of the classic entrepreneurial owner-managed firm. A small organization is a simple yet dynamic environment which can be understood by one leading individual. 'Most organizations pass through the Simple Structure in their formative years', and some stay small enough to continue it. They could be as diverse as an automobile dealership, a retail store, a brand-new government department, or a vigorous manufacturer on a small scale.

Some people enjoy working in such an organization because of the sense of mission it gives, and its flexibility. Others resent the domination from the top. They see it as paternalistic or autocratic, unfashionable in democratic times. The organization is also precarious: 'one heart attack can literally wipe out the organization's prime coordinating mechanism'.

The *Machine Bureaucracy* is far more secure (see Weber on bureaucracy, p. 7). It does not depend on a single person. The strongest pull on it is from its *technostructure*, the planners, financial controllers, production schedulers, and their kind. They pull towards standardization. Once work has been divided into standard routine tasks it can be controlled by them through formalized rules and regulations. Control is almost an obsession. The Machine Bureaucracy is second only to the Simple Structure in centralization, but in it power is divided between the strategic apex and the technostructure. A post office, a steel manufacturer, a prison, a major airline, a vehicle assembler, are all like this. They have the conditions favouring this design, mainly that they are older larger organizations carrying out repetitive work in stable environments, probably themselves subject to control from a remote corporation head office or government.

Though efficient at repetitive work, this form of organization is riddled with conflict between top and bottom and between departments. To many of its personnel the work they do is meaningless. Its managers spend much of their energy just holding it together. It was fashionable at the height of the industrial revolution, but like the Simple Structure it is no longer so.

The third kind of configuration or design, the *Professional Bureaucracy*, is pulled by its *operating core* towards professionalized autonomy. That is, it is dominated by highly trained professional specialists. These have to be employed because the work is too complex to be controlled and coordinated any other way. So it is broken up into specialisms, and people are hired to do it who already have standardized skills. That means professionals already trained and indoctrinated who can be relied on to do what has to be done. This is the situation in universities, hospitals, schools, accountancy firms, social work agencies, and some firms that employ highly skilled craftspeople (e.g. in fashion textiles designing). Since others without the training cannot interfere, the professionals are relatively independent. Their working autonomy is usually reinforced by a high demand for the service they give. Hence whilst the Machine Bureaucracy is run by hierarchical authority, the Professional Bureaucracy emphasizes the power of expertise. While the Machine Bureaucracy sets its own standards, the bureaucratic administrative framework of a Professional Bureaucracy accepts standards set externally by professional bodies such as the medical and accounting institutions.

This design of organization is uniquely democratic, but it suffers from difficulties of coordination and jurisdiction. Who should teach the statistics course in the management degree, the staff of the mathematics department or the business department? And who can declare a professor incompetent, and what then can be done about it?

The *Divisionalized Form* is most widely used by large private industrial corporations, but it can also be seen in those American universities that have several campuses, or in health administrations which control several hospitals, and generally in socialist economies where government ministries control numbers of enterprises. It 'piggybacks on the Machine Bureaucracy', for it is a headquarters controlling several Machine Bureaucracies. These make a powerful *middle line*, in Mintzberg's terminology, the key part around which the organization functions. It is pulled towards Balkanization, for each division is relatively self-sufficient with its own marketing, purchasing and manufacturing (or equivalent) and so on, and each operates in its own market. Indeed, the Divisionalized Form is usually the result of a Machine Bureaucracy diversifying across more than one market, either into different products or into different geographical areas.

Though each division has a great deal of autonomy, headquarters decides how much capital each shall have and watches numerical performance indicators such as profits, sales and return on investment. This is where the problems arise. Headquarters may meddle too much in divisional decisions, and its concentration on numerical indicators may neglect other considerations such as product quality or environmental preservation. Mintzberg suspects that though the Divisionalized Form is a fashionable sign of the times, it may be the most vulnerable of the five designs to legal and social changes.

In contrast, a space agency, an avant-garde film company, a factory making complex prototypes, or a petrochemicals company, is likely to be designed as an *Adhocracy*. These are young research-based organizations which need to innovate in rapidly changing conditions. The primary key part of an Adhocracy is the *support staff* in research and development, but there may be also key *operating core* personnel, experts on whom innovation depends. Unlike the Professional Bureaucracy, the Adhocracy is not seeking the repetitive use of professionally standardized skills. Instead, it groups its highly trained specialists in mixed project teams, hoping to generate new ideas. It is pulled towards coordination within and between teams by 'mutual adjustment' (see Thompson, p. 51), i.e. by direct cooperation. Unified bureaucratic controls might get in the way. Of the five designs of organization, 'Adhocracy shows the least reverence for the classical principles of management' (e.g. as promulgated by Fayol, p. 85). It is uniquely both organic and decentralized.

There are two variants of Adhocracy. An Operating Adhocracy works directly for clients, as in an advertising agency, whereas an Administrative Bureaucracy serves itself, as did the National Aeronautics and Space Agency, NASA, in building up American space exploration.

Inevitably, Adhocracy creates difficulties as well as innovations. People talk a lot, and this costs time. There is confusion over who is doing what. It is the most politicized design, breeding internal competition and conflict. Yet 'if Simple Structure and Machine Bureaucracy were yesterday's structures, and Professional Bureaucracy and the Divisionalized Form are today's, then Adhocracy is clearly tomorrow's'.

It may not be the only one. Mintzberg speculates about another structure of the future, in which ideology is important. Perhaps it can be seen in the Israeli kibbutzim and in Japanese manufacturing. He calls it the Missionary. Indeed, organizations approximate one of his main five types only when one 'pull' is strongest. If two or more 'pulls' balance then hybrids emerge. So as organizations search for structures that are in harmony internally and with their environments, new varieties are always possible.

BIBLIOGRAPHY

MINTZBERG, H., *The Nature of Managerial Work*, Harper & Row, 1973; Prentice-Hall, 1980.

MINTZBERG, H., 'The Manager's Job: Folklore and Fact.' *Harvard Business Review*, (1975), 49–61; reprinted in D. S. Pugh (ed.), *Organization Theory*, Penguin, 1990.

MINTZBERG, H., *The Structuring of Organizations*, Prentice-Hall, 1979.

MINTZBERG, H., *Structures in Fives: Designing Effective Organizations*, Prentice-Hall, 1983.

2 The Organization in its Environment

The beginning of administrative wisdom is the awareness that there is no one optimum type of management system.
TOM BURNS

The effective organization has integrating devices consistent with the diversity of its environment. The more diverse the environment and the more differentiated the organization, the more elaborate the integrating devices.
PAUL LAWRENCE and JAY LORSCH

Uncertainties pose major challenges to rationality.
JAMES D. THOMPSON

The key to organizational survival is the ability to acquire and maintain resources.
JEFFREY PFEFFER and GERALD R. SALANCIK

Efficient organizations establish mechanisms that complement their market strategy.
RAYMOND E. MILES and CHARLES C. SNOW

An ecology of organizations seeks to understand how social conditions affect the rates at which new organizations and new organizational forms arise, the rates at which organizations change forms, and the rates at which organizations and forms die out.
MICHAEL T. HANNAN and JOHN FREEMAN

Transaction cost economizing is, we submit, the driving force that is responsible for the main institutional changes [in corporations].
OLIVER E. WILLIAMSON

Whether they like it or not the headquarters of multinationals are in the business of multicultural management.
GEERT HOFSTEDE

All organizations are situated in an environment, be that, for example, business, governmental, educational or voluntary service. In this environment are other organizations and people with whom transactions have to take place. These will include suppliers, clients or customers, and competitors. In addition there will be more general aspects of the environment which will have important effects, such as legal, technological and ethical developments.

The writers in this section have been concerned to analyse how the need to function successfully in different environments has led organizations to adopt different structures and strategies. Tom Burns examines the effects of rapidly changing technological developments on the attempts of old-fashioned firms to adjust to new environments. Paul Lawrence and Jay Lorsch emphasize that it is the appropriateness of the organization's structure in relation to its environmental requirements which is the basis of effectiveness.

James D. Thompson portrays organizations as open systems having to achieve their goals in the face of uncertainty in their environments. Jeffrey Pfeffer and Gerald Salancik argue for a 'resource dependence perspective' which sees all organizational functioning as resulting from the organization's interdependence with its environment. Raymond Miles and Charles Snow emphasize the strategic choices that managements have to make to adapt to the environmental pressures they face, while Michael Hannan and John Freeman take an ecological and evolutionary view of the chances of organizations surviving in their particular environments.

Oliver E. Williamson suggests the circumstances in which the organization's transactions with its environment are based on market relationships, and those where they are incorporated into hierarchical planning mechanisms. Geert Hofstede highlights national culture as it affects management values and processes. This environmental feature is particularly important in the ever more frequent international activities of organizations.

Tom Burns

Tom Burns spent more than thirty years at the university of Edinburgh, retiring in 1981 as Professor of Sociology. His early interests were in urban sociology and he worked with the West Midland Group on Post-war Reconstruction and Planning. While he was at Edinburgh his particular concern was with studies of different types of organization and their effects on communication patterns and on the activities of managers. He has also explored the relevance of different forms of organization to changing conditions – especially to the impact of technical innovation.

In collaboration with a psychologist (G. M. Stalker), Burns has studied the attempt to introduce electronics development work into traditional Scottish firms, with a view to their entering this modern and rapidly expanding industry as the markets for their own well-established products diminished. The difficulties which these firms faced in adjusting to the new situation of continuously changing technology and markets led him to describe two 'ideal types' of management organization which are the extreme points of a continuum along which most organizations can be placed.

The *mechanistic* type of organization is adapted to relatively stable conditions. In it the problems and tasks of management are broken down into specialisms within which each individual carries out his assigned, precisely defined, task. There is a clear hierarchy of control, and the responsibility for overall knowledge and coordination rests exclusively at the top of the hierarchy. Vertical communication and interaction (i.e. between superiors and subordinates) is emphasized, and there is an insistence on loyalty to the concern and obedience to superiors. This system corresponds quite closely to Weber's rational–legal bureaucracy (see p. 7).

The *organismic* (also called *organic*) type of organization is adapted to unstable conditions when new and unfamiliar problems continually arise which cannot be broken down and distributed among the existing specialist roles. There is therefore a continual adjustment and redefinition of individual tasks and the contributive rather then restrictive nature of specialist knowledge is emphasized. Interactions and communication (information and advice rather than orders) may occur at any level as required by the process, and a much higher degree of commitment to the aims of the organization as a whole is generated. In this system, organization charts laying down the exact functions and responsibilities of each individual are not found, and indeed their use may be explicitly rejected as hampering the efficient functioning of the organization.

The almost complete failure of the traditional Scottish firms to absorb electronics research and development engineers into their organizations leads Burns to doubt whether a mechanistic firm can consciously change to an organismic one. This is because individuals in a mechanistic organization are not only committed to the organization as a whole, but are also members of a group or department with a stable career structure and with sectional interests in conflict with those of other groups. Thus there develop power struggles between established sections to obtain control of the new functions and resources. These divert the organization from purposive adaptation and allow out-of-date mechanistic structures to be perpetuated and 'pathological' systems to develop.

Pathological systems are attempts by mechanistic organizations to cope with new problems of change, innovation and uncertainty while sticking to the formal bureaucratic structure. Burns describes three of these typical reactions. In a mechanistic organization the normal procedure for dealing with a matter outside an individual's sphere of responsibility is to refer it to the appropriate specialist or, failing that, to a superior. In a rapidly changing situation the need for such consultations occurs frequently; and in many instances the superior has to put up the matter higher still. A heavy load of such decisions finds its way to the chief executive, and it soon becomes apparent that many decisions can only be made by going to the top. Thus there develops the *ambiguous figure system* of an official hierarchy and a non-officially-recognised system of pair relationships between the chief executive and some dozens of people at different positions in the management structure. The head of the concern is overloaded with work, and many senior managers whose status depends on the functioning of the formal system feel frustrated at being by-passed.

Some firms attempted to cope with the problems of communication by creating more branches of the bureaucratic hierarchy e.g. contract managers, liaison officers. This leads to a system described as the *mechanistic jungle*, in which a new job or even a whole new department may be created, whose existence depends on the perpetuation of these difficulties. The third type of pathological response is the *super-personal* or *committee system*. The committee is the traditional way of dealing with temporary problems which cannot be solved within a single individual's role without upsetting the balance of power. But as a permanent device it is inefficient, in that it has to compete with the loyalty demanded and career structure offered by the traditional departments. This system was tried only sporadically by the firms, since it was disliked as being typical of inefficient government administration; attempts to develop the committee as a super-person to fulfil a continuing function that no individual could carry out met with little success.

For a proper understanding of organizational functioning, Burns maintains, it is therefore always necessary to conceive of organizations as the simultaneous working of at least three social systems. The first of these is the formal authority system derived from the aims of the organization, its technology, its attempts to cope with its environment. This is the overt system in terms of which all discussion about decision-making takes place. But organizations are also cooperative systems of people who have career aspirations and a career structure, and who compete for advancement. Thus decisions taken in the overt structure inevitably affect the differential career prospects of the members, who will therefore evaluate them in terms of the career system as well as the formal system, and will react accordingly. This leads to the third system of relationships which is part of an organization – its political system. Every organization is the scene of 'political' activity in which individuals and departments compete and cooperate for power. Again all decisions in the overt system are evaluated for their relative impact on the power structure as well as for their contribution to the achievement of the organization's goals.

It is naive to consider the organization as a unitary system equated with the formal system, and any change to be successful must be acceptable in terms of the career structure and the political structure as well. This is particularly so with modern technologically based organizations which contain qualified experts who have a career structure and a technical authority which goes far beyond the organization itself and its top management. Thus the attempt to change from a mechanistic to an organismic management structure has enormous implications for the career structure (which is much less dependent on the particular organization) and the power system (which is much more diffuse deriving from technical knowledge as much as formal position).

Concern with the interaction of these three social systems within the organization continues in Burns's study of the British Broadcasting Corporation. The BBC is a very segmented organization both horizontally, where there are a large number of departments (e.g. Drama, Outside Broadcasts, Finance) who appear to be competing as much as cooperating, and vertically, where in order to rise in the grading structure executives soon lose contact with the professional skills (e.g. journalism, engineering) which they are supposed to administer. In this situation the career and the political systems can become more important than the formal task system.

Burns charts the rise in power of the central management of the BBC at the expense of the creative and professional staff, which stems from the Corporation's financial pressures. He maintains that the Corporation can only develop as a creative service dedicated to the public good, if it is freed from its financial client relationship to the government.

'A sense of the past and the very recent past is essential to anyone who is trying to perceive the here-and-now of industrial organization.' If the organizational structure is viewed as a result of a process of continuous development of the three social systems of formal organization, career structure and political system, a study of this process will help organizations to avoid traps they would otherwise fall into. Adaptation to new and changing situations is not automatic. Indeed many factors militate against it. An important one is the existence of an organization structure appropriate to an earlier phase of development. Another is the multifaceted nature of the commitments of organizational members: to their careers, their departments, their specialist sub-units. These are often stronger than their commitment to the organization as a whole.

BIBLIOGRAPHY

BURNS, T., 'Industry in a new age', *New Society*, 31 January 1963, no. 18; reprinted in D. S. PUGH (ed.), *Organization Theory*, Penguin, 1990.

BURNS, T., 'On the plurality of social systems' in J. R. LAWRENCE (ed.), *Operational Research and the Social Sciences*, Tavistock, 1966.

BURNS, T., *The BBC: Public Institution and Private World*, Macmillan, 1977.

BURNS, T., and STALKER, G. M., *The Management of Innovation*, Tavistock, 1961, 2nd edn 1968.

Paul Lawrence and Jay Lorsch

Paul Lawrence and Jay Lorsch are professorial colleagues in Organizational Behaviour at the Harvard Business School, where Lawrence has taught for over forty years and Lorsch since 1965. Together with many collaborators (who include S. A. Allan, S. M. Davis, J. Kotter, H. Lane, and J. J. Morse) they have for two decades been conducting a series of studies into the appropriate structure and functioning of organizations using what has become known as the 'organization and environment' approach, described in their seminal book of that title.

Lawrence and Lorsch begin their analysis with the question of why people seek to build organizations. Their answer is that organizations enable people to find better solutions to the environmental problems facing them. This immediately highlights three key elements in their approach to understanding organizational behaviour (1) it is people who have purposes, not organizations; (2) people have to come together to coordinate their different activities into an organization; and (3) the effectiveness of the organization is judged by the adequacy with which the members' needs are satisfied through planned transactions with the environment.

It is in order to cope effectively with their external environments that organizations must come to develop segmented units, each of which has as its major task the problem of dealing with some aspect of the conditions outside the firm. For example, in a manufacturing firm with production, sales and design units, the production unit deals with production equipment sources, raw materials sources and labour markets; the sales unit faces problems with the market, the customers and the competitors; the design unit has to cope with technological developments, government regulations and so on. This *differentiation* of function and task is accompanied by differences in cognitive and emotional orientation among the managers in different units, and differences too, in the formal structure of different departments. For instance the development department may have a long-term horizon and a very informal structure, whereas production may be dealing with day-to-day problems in a rigidly formal system, with sales facing the medium-term effects of competitors' advertising with moderate formality.

In spite of this the organization is a system which has to be coordinated so that a state of collaboration exists in order to reap the benefits of effective transactions with the environment. This is the required *integration* and it, too, is affected by the nature of the external conditions.

The basic necessity for *both* appropriate differentiation *and* adequate integration to perform effectively in the external environment is at the core of Lawrence and Lorsch's model of organizational functioning. The approach was developed in an important study which they carried out on ten firms in three different industries – plastics (six firms), food (two firms) and containers (two firms) – which constituted very different environments for the enterprises concerned.

The study recognized that all the firms involved segment their environment. Each of the ten was dealing with a market sub-environment (the task of the sales department), a techno-economic sub-environment (the task of the manufacturing unit) and a scientific sub-environment (the task of the R&D or design department). The greater the degree of uncertainty within each sub-environment and the greater the diversity between them, the greater was the need of the firms to *differentiate* between their sub-units of sales, production and research in order to be effective in each sub-environment. For example in the plastics industry, which was found to have great diversity, with the science sub-environment highly uncertain but the techno-economic one relatively stable, a considerable degree of differentiation within effective firms was found. In the container industry, on the other hand, all parts of the environment were relatively certain and so a much lower degree of differentiation was apparent.

But greater differentiation brings with it potential for greater inter-departmental conflict as the specialist groups develop their own ways of dealing with the particular uncertainties of their own sub-environments. These differences are not just minor variations in outlook but may involve fundamental ways of thinking and behaving. In the plastics industry a sales manager may be discussing a potential new product in terms of whether it will perform in the customers' machinery, whether they will pay the cost and whether it can be got on to the market in three months' time. The research scientist at the same meeting may be thinking about whether the molecular structure of the material could be changed without affecting its stability and whether doing this would open out a line of research for the next two years which would be more interesting than other projects. These two specialists not only think differently, they dress differently, they have different habits of punctuality and so on. It therefore becomes crucial that a highly differentiated firm should have appropriate methods of *integration* and conflict resolution if they are to perform well in the environment.

The table below lists the integrative devices which were found to be operating in three high-performing organizations, one from each of the industries studied. The top row gives the rating for the degree of differentiation, and it will be seen that the need to operate effectively in the plastics environment led the firm to develop a high degree of differentiation; the container firm had the lowest differentiation and the food firm was in between.

Comparison of Integrative Devices in Three High-performing Organizations

	Plastics	*Food*	*Container*
Degree of differentiation	10.7	8.0	5.7
Major integrative devices	(1) Integrative department	(1) Individual integrators	(1) Direct managerial contact
	(2) Permanent cross-functional teams at three levels of management	(2) Temporary cross-functional teams	(2) Managerial hierarchy
	(3) Direct managerial contact	(3) Direct managerial contact	(3) Paper system
	(4) Managerial hierarchy	(4) Managerial hierarchy	
	(5) Paper system	(5) Paper system	

from Lawrence and Lorsch (1967)

Each of these firms used a different combination of devices for achieving integration. All of them used to some extent the traditional methods of paper systems, the formal managerial hierarchy and direct managerial contact between members of the different departments. For the container firm with the least differentiation these methods were sufficient but in the food firm, which had a greater need for integration, temporary teams made up of specialists from the units involved were set up to deal with any particularly urgent issue. Managers within functional departments were also assigned integrating roles such as that of liaison officer. Clearly the effective food firm was devoting a larger amount of time and effort to integrating activity.

The plastics organization had in addition established a special department one of whose primary activities was integration. They also had an elaborate set of permanent integrating teams, each made up of members from the various functional units and the integrating department. The purpose of these teams was to provide a formal setting in which interdepartmental conflicts such as the one described above between the sales manager and the research scientist could be resolved with the help of an integrator. The effective plastics firm drew on the whole range of integrative devices and needed to do so because its necessary differentiation was so high.

It is the appropriateness of the three-way relationships between the uncertainty and diversity of the environment, the degree of organizational differentiation, and the state of integration and conflict resolution achieved, which will lead to effective functioning. Inadequacy in any of these relationships was associated with lower performance. Thus, for example, the high performers in the plastics and food industry had *both* greater differentiation *and* greater integration than the low performers, since both were required. By contrast, in the low-performing container organization there was no evidence that the integrating unit it possessed was serving a useful purpose given its low level of differentiation.

Effective conflict resolution, which is the behavioural basis of integration, was found to have a pattern in which inter-unit conflict is dealt with by managers working in a problem-solving mode to face the issues and work through to the best overall solution – rather than smoothing over the issues to avoid conflict, or letting the party with the greater power force its solution on others. It was also found that in dealing with conflict effectively, the individuals primarily involved in achieving integration (whether they be superiors in the line hierarchy, or persons appointed specifically to coordinating roles) need to have their authority based not just on their formal position, but largely on their knowledge of and competence on the issues as perceived by all the groups involved, together with a balanced orientation between the parties. The power and influence to make decisions leading to the resolution of conflict must therefore be located at the points where the knowledge to reach such decisions also exists.

The Lawrence and Lorsch framework, by emphasizing that the appropriate organization structure will depend upon the environmental demands, takes a 'contingency' approach, rejecting the formulation that one particular structural form (e.g. bureaucracy, see Weber, p. 7) or one particular motivational approach (e.g. Theory Y, see McGregor, p. 156) is always best. It is the appropriateness which is the key.

Lorsch and Morse in a further study compared two manufacturing plants (one high-performing, one low-performing) with two research laboratories (similarly high and low performers). The organization structures and processes of the high-performing manufacturer in a relatively certain environment were: high formality, short time-horizon, highly directive management. The individuals working in this organization were found to have low cognitive complexity, low tolerance for ambiguity, and dependency in authority relationships. The high-performing research laboratory in a relatively uncertain environment had low formality, long time-horizons and high participation. Its members had high cognitive complexity, high tolerance for ambiguity and independence in authority relationships. Yet both organizations were effective because they were appropriately organized with appropriate members for their environmental tasks. Indeed the less effective organization in each pair did not show most of the distinctive characteristics of structure and process to the same degree. On the other hand the characteristics of the members were as clearly differentiated as in the successful organizations. These less effective organizations, it seems, could obtain the appropriate people but not organize them in the appropriate way. But equally, in other cases failure could be due to having inappropriate people even though they were appropriately organized.

In a later study of seven major U S industries, including those of steel, agriculture, hospitals and telecommunication, Lawrence and Dyer developed the 'competitive principle'. This maintains that an industry needs to experience an appropriate degree of vigorous competition in its environment if it is to be economically strong. Either too little or too much competition will lead to inefficient and non-innovative performance. They argue for the setting up of a government agency to monitor the competitive pressures in each industry to determine whether they need to be increased or reduced.

The analysis of matrix organizations has been a particular concern of Davis and Lawrence. Matrix organization structures are those in which there is a multiple command system – many managers having two bosses. For example, finance managers would have a finance director to whom they would be responsible for professional standards, and who would be concerned with their career development and promotion. In addition each would also report to a project director to whom they would be responsible for giving the appropriate cost accounting services needed for their current project, and who would therefore be in charge of the day-to-day work allocation. Clearly this form of structure violates Fayol's principle of 'unity of command' (see p. 85) and its greater complexity would be the preferred structure only in certain situations. These are when (1) there are several highly salient sectors (i.e. products, markets, functions etc.) which are simultaneously necessary for goal achievement; (2) the tasks are uncertain, complex and interdependent; and (3) there is a need to realize economies by using scarce resources effectively. In these circumstances, there is a need for complex differentiation and integration via the matrix mode.

BIBLIOGRAPHY

LAWRENCE, P. R., and LORSCH J. W., *Organization and Environment*, Harvard, 1967.

LAWRENCE, P. R. and LORSCH, J. W., *Developing Organizations: Diagnosis and Action*, Addison-Wesley, 1969.

LORSCH, J. W. and MORSE, J. J., *Organizations and Their Members: A Contingency Approach*, Harper & Row, 1974.

DAVIS, S. M. and LAWRENCE, P. R., *Matrix*, Addison-Wesley, 1977.

DONALDSON, G., and LORSCH, J.W., *Decison Making at the Top*, Basic Books, 1983.

LAWRENCE. P. R., and DYER, D., *Renewing American Industry*, Free Press, 1983.

James D. Thompson

After leaving the American armed forces subsequent to the Second World War, James Thompson (1920–73) became a sociologist. Yet he made his contribution to the understanding of organizations through research in business schools. He was the founding editor of the world's leading research journal in organization theory, the *Administrative Science Quarterly*. He died prematurely only six years after the publication in 1967 of his classic book *Organizations in Action*. This book draws together a range of ideas which were forming at the time it was written, and which have continued to be at the centre of organization theory. It is a portrayal of complex organizations 'as open systems, hence indeterminate and faced with uncertainty, but at the same time as subject to criteria of rationality and hence needing determinateness and certainty'. It pictures organizations continually striving to act rationally in the face of technological and environmental uncertainties. Their basic problem is how to cope with these uncertainties.

In other words, organizations – or rather, their members – aspire to be reasoned and orderly despite circumstances and events which may prevent them being so. These standards, or *norms of rationality* to which they aspire, demand of organizations both coordination within, and adjustment without. The twin tasks of administration are to provide the needful coordination within the organization and the adjustment to circumstances outside it.

The first task therefore is to achieve the stable coordination of those basic work activities which Thompson calls the *technical core* of an organization. For example, in factory production work, supplies of components must be continuously in the right places at the right times if assembly is to proceed smoothly, just as in a college the teachers and students must be in the right rooms at the right times.

The second task of administration is to regulate transactions across the boundary of the organization, that is its contacts with the world outside itself. This might be done by negotiating with outside interests for, say, assured financial credit, or raw materials, or by changing with the environment, as when a chain of toy stores changes what it sells in response to rising public standards of safety for children. Or it might be done by *buffering*. Buffering protects the technical core from the uncertainties of acquiring resources, and of disposing of outputs (e.g. by having a purchasing department to handle suppliers and a sales department to deal with customers). A public relations department can cope with challenges to the rightfulness of what the organization is doing, as in the cases of nuclear power or cigarette manufacture. Such *boundary spanning units* are placed between the technical core and the outside world to buffer it from external shocks. Another possibility is to move the boundaries of the organization to encircle sources of uncertainty and bring them under control, for instance to ensure supplies by buying up a supplier firm.

Hence organizations come to be made up of a variety of different parts. These can be linked together in fundamentally different ways, and so internal interdependence may differ from one organization to the next, and within any one organization. Interdependence can be pooled, sequential, or reciprocal. *Pooled interdependence* is where the work of each part of an organization is not directly connected to that of the others but is a 'discrete contribution to the whole'. Yet since each is supported by that whole organization, which in turn would be threatened by the failure of any of its parts, they have a pooled interdependence within it. Such is the situation in a university where the departments of biology, French language, and management, for example, are not linked in any way other than by their common reliance upon the university as a whole.

In *sequential interdependence* one part cannot do its job until others have done theirs. Tasks have to be done in sequence, first this, then that. Such is the situation in a factory where one workshop must machine components to the right sizes before the next can put them through a hardening treatment, and so on through successive stages up to the final product.

In *reciprocal interdependence* each does something for the other. Unlike the one way flow in sequential interdependence, the outputs of both become inputs for the other. That is the situation in an airline where the flight operations section constantly makes aircraft available to the maintenance engineers for servicing, and the engineers constantly turn out aircraft ready for the operations people to fly.

Reciprocal interdependence requires the closest coordination, sequential interdependence less, pooled interdependence least. While all organizations have a certain amount of pooled interdependence, and in some it may be the prevalent form, not all have sequential interdependence in addition to pooled, and fewer still have within them all these kinds of interdependence.

The various units are grouped in the hierarchy of an organization in such a way as to minimize the costs of coordinating what they do. The means of coordination differ. Reciprocally interdependent units have to coordinate what each does for the other by *mutual adjustment*, so they are likely to be placed together in the hierarchy under common superiors who can ensure that they cooperate. If units are sequentially interdependent, then their work can be coordinated by *planning or scheduling*, the work of each being planned to dovetail in sequence with that of the next in line. In a factory, a prior department in the sequence has to turn out enough components so that the next department in the sequence is not left standing idle. If there is merely pooled interdependence, then some coordination within the whole can be achieved by *standardization* of the rules which link each part with the whole: in a university, for example, though the departments differ in their contributions to the whole, in principle they are all to be dealt with in the same manner when it comes to examination procedures or budget allocations (which is not to say that they all get the same budget).

Organizations also differ in the activities undertaken by their technical core. They have one or more of three technologies. A *long-linked technology*, as in manufacturing, performs a series of tasks in a set order, giving rise to the sequential interdependence of units referred to earlier. A *mediating technology* links other parties, as where banks mediate between lenders and borrowers or an employment agency mediates between prospective employers and employees. Thirdly, an *intensive technology* functions in response to feedback from the object worked upon, as where what is done and when it is done depend in a hospital upon the patient's condition, or at a construction site upon the condition of the ground.

The ways in which organizations attempt to encircle external sources of uncertainty by extending their boundaries are determined by these kinds of technology. Those with long-linked technologies tend to go for a corresponding vertical integration, as when oil refiners own roadside service stations and automobile manufacturers own suppliers of components. Those with mediating technologies try to increase the populations they serve, so that airlines increase their route networks and banks put branches into new areas. Finally, organizations with intensive technology attempt to incorporate the object worked upon so as to control it better, for instance universities making their students also their members and therefore subject to their rules, or mental hospitals bringing patients inside for observation.

This extension of boundaries is not the only way of coping with environmentally derived uncertainty. As also mentioned before, organizations can buffer their technical core by setting up boundary spanning units which allow the core to operate as if there were stability. By stockpiling supplies and outputs, for example, work can continue as if there were a steady stream of supplies and a steady demand by the market. Alternatively, fluctuations may be prevented, as when utilities offer cheap off-peak gas or electricity to smooth out demand, or may be anticipated, as when ice cream production is adjusted to seasonal changes. If buffering, smoothing and anticipating fail, organizations can resort to rationing. So the post office gives priority to first class mail, a hospital may deal only with urgent cases and a manufacturer may limit the proportion of popular items taken by any one wholesaler.

The relation between technical core and boundary spanning activities gives rise to appropriate types of structure. Where technical core and boundary spanning activities can be isolated from one another, there is likely to be in the hierarchy a layer of functionally specialized departments such as purchasing and sales and finance, comparatively remote from the core and under central control. Where core and boundary activities are more closely interdependent, there is more likely to be a divisionalized structure, decentralized into 'self-sufficient clusters' of units. Each cluster has only so much to deal with, for instance as in a divisionalized multinational firm which has one multi-department division covering Europe, another covering South East Asia, and so on.

Norms of rationality, which Thompson repeatedly stresses are assumed in all that he has to say about organizations, require that organizations 'keep score' so that their performances can be assessed. The problem is how to do this. Where it is possible to trace clearly the consequences of what is done (i.e. where there is a clear presumption that new equipment has reduced costs) then efficiency measures can be used. These assume understanding of cause and effect, and known standards of performance, as is the case with many financial indicators in industry. However, if *intrinsic criteria* which indicate relatively directly the standard of work done are lacking, then *extrinsic criteria* have to be used. From these the quantity and quality of the work can be inferred but they do not show it directly. Hence university research is measured by counting the money gained for it in competitive applications to funding institutions, and by the number of publications about it, rather than by its results as such, and mental hospitals emphasize discharge rates rather than the extent to which patients are cured.

Organizations are torn between the differing assessments made by a variety of assessors. The potential users of a public health service will look at it in one way, the government providing the money will look at it in another. The users are concerned with the treatment given, the government is concerned more with the cost of the treatment. Shareholders stress dividend and profits, customers stress prices. So each organization tries to do best on the criteria used by those on whom it is most dependent. Furthermore, it will try to score well on the most *visible criteria.* These are the most obvious to the most important assessors. Business firms are sensitive to the price of their stock on the stock exchange, schools announce the examination performances of top pupils, and so on. Less visible criteria may be neglected, even if they are intrinsically more desirable.

According to Thompson, the more sources of uncertainty there are the more possibilities there are for gaining power (see also Crozier p. 138), and the more likely it is that 'political' positions will be taken up. In general individuals higher in management have discretion in decisions and so what should be done is subject to their personal judgement, including their assessment of what will be acceptable to others. This political assessment would be crucial in deciding, for example, whether or not two departments could be successfully merged.

The making of decisions involves beliefs, or assumptions, as to what will happen if this is done rather than that, and preferences as to what is most desirable. There is less certainty about some beliefs and preferences than there is about others, as illustrated by Thompson's matrix:

		Preferences regarding possible outcomes	
		Certainty	Uncertainty
Beliefs about cause/effect relations	Certain	COMPUTATIONAL STRATEGY	COMPROMISE STRATEGY
	Uncertain	JUDGEMENTAL STRATEGY	INSPIRATIONAL STRATEGY

The matrix shows four likely kinds of *decision-making strategies.* The two left-hand boxes represent situations where there is relative certainty on what is wanted. Those concerned are clear on what outcome they prefer. In the top left-hand box they are also certain of what the consequences of their decision may be. Such all-round certainty might occur if they were considering increasing existing production capacity in response to a steady rise in sales. Agreed on the need to expand, and knowing the technology from past experience, management could confidently calculate likely costs and returns in a *computational* manner. However, the lower box represents a situation where cause and effect are less well known. Here the same management still wants to expand capacity but if they do they will have to buy new machinery of an untried design. This decision is less susceptible to computation, more a *judgemental* matter assessing the risk involved.

In the two right-hand boxes, managers are not sure what they want and there may be divided opinions. Alternative outcomes may each be attractive, for instance increasing capacity either for mass production of low quality products, or for a smaller volume of higher quality products. If the technology for both is well known, and market forecasts are confident that either can be profitable, a *compromise* strategy results in some of each. However, if there is all-round uncertainty as in the lower right-hand box, then an *inspirational strategy* is more likely. There are neither clear preferences for high volume against low volume production, nor is there confidence in what the consequences of new production machinery or of launching more goods on to the market will be. The strategy has to be an inspired leap in the dark.

In Thompson's view, the aim of management and administration when designing organizations and making decisions must be the effective alignment of organization structure, technology and environment. This central conception has been and continues to be at the heart of organization theory, and it is a constant stimulus to research. Again and again his analysis is returned to as a source of ideas, few of which have been as yet supplanted.

BIBLIOGRAPHY

THOMPSON, J. D., *Organizations in Action*, McGraw-Hill, 1967

Jeffrey Pfeffer and Gerald R. Salancik

Jeffrey Pfeffer and Gerald Salancik are respectively professors at the Stanford University Graduate School of Business, California, and the Department of Business Administration, University of Illinois. Pfeffer and Salancik contend that organizations should be understood in terms of their interdependence with their environments. They advocate a *resource dependence perspective*. For example, explaining discontent among the employees of a fast-food chain by poor human relations and poor pay is irrelevant if the organization can draw on a pool of easily recruited youthful labour, and since its competitors can do so too, the organization is not going to incur the costs of better human relations and pay.

Organizations are not self-directed and autonomous. They need resources, including money, materials, personnel and information, and to get these they must interact with others who control the resources. This involves them in a constant struggle for autonomy as they confront external constraints. They become 'quasi-markets' in which influence is bartered not only between internal sections but between those sections or sub-units and external interests.

Interdependence with others lies in the availability of resources and the demand for them. It is of many kinds. For instance, there is the direct dependence of a seller organization upon its customers, and there is the indirect dependence upon each other of two seller organizations, not in mutual contact, via a set of potential customers for whom they compete.

Three conditions define how dependent an organization is. First is the importance of a resource to it. This is a combination of the magnitude of that resource (in other words, the proportion of inputs and outputs accounted for by the resource), and of its criticality, best revealed by how severe the consequences would be if it were not available. Second is how much discretion those who control a resource have over its allocation and use. If they have completely free access to it and can make the rules about it, then an organization which needs it can be put in a highly dependent position. Third is how far those who control a resource have a monopoly of it. Can an organization which needs it find an alternative source or a substitute? Thus 'the potential for one organization's influencing another derives from its discretionary control over resources needed by that other, and the other's dependence on the resource and lack of countervailing resources or access to alternative sources'. Since the others on whom an organization depends may not be dependable, its effectiveness is indicated more by how well it balances these dependencies than by internal measures of efficiency of a financial or similar nature.

To Pfeffer and Salancik the possible strategies that an organization may use to balance its dependencies are of four kinds. It may:

1. Adapt to or alter constraints.
2. Alter the interdependencies by merger, diversification, or growth.
3. Negotiate its environment by interlocking directorships or joint ventures with other organizations or by other associations.
4. Change the legality or legitimacy of its environment by political action.

There are numerous ways of carrying out the first kind of strategy, adapting to or altering external constraints. An organization can pay sequential attention (see March, p. 123) to the demands made upon it, attending first to one and then to another as in turn they become more pressing. For example, for a time customers may take priority, then attention may switch to financial economies required by owners or lenders. An organization can play one interest off against another (e.g. blaming different unions for current difficulties). It can influence the formulation of demands (e.g. by advertising); it can claim that it cannot comply because of, say, legal restrictions; it can minimise its dependence by stocks of materials or money. And so on.

Merging, diversifying or growing are each ways of pursuing the second kind of strategy, altering the interdependent relationships. Mergers do this by bringing control of critical resources within one organization, stabilizing the exchanges of which they are part. They may be backwards, sideways, or forwards, incorporating suppliers, competitors, or purchasers. Diversification shifts and widens the interdependencies in which an organization is enmeshed, extricating it from over-dependence in any one field. Growth in size increases the power of an organization relative to others, and makes more people interested in its survival. Size has been found to improve stability more than profitability.

Third, negotiating the environment is a more common strategy than total absorption by merger. Interlocking directorships, whereby boards include members of the boards of other organizations, cartels to control supplies, trade agreements, memberships in trade associations and coordinating industry councils and advisory bodies, joint ventures in which two or more organizations work together, and the like, are commonplace. Such links help to keep the participating organizations informed about what is happening outside themselves, and to ensure mutual commitment. Normative expectations build up as to what each other will do, making each more sure of the other's reliability.

Fourth, and finally, if none of the other strategies are open to them organizations resort to political action. They endeavour to obtain and sustain favourable taxation, or tariffs, or subsidies, or licensing of themselves or their members (as where the practice of medicine or law, for example, is restricted to defined categories of qualified people), or they charge others with violating regulations (as when competitors are accused of prohibited monopolistic arrangements). There is constant political activity by organizations which give to political party funds, lobby the members of legislatures, and are represented on governmental and related agencies and councils. Indeed, if there is a high level of state regulation, the decisions of lawmakers and government agencies become more important to an organization than those of its customers or clients.

How are the effects of the environment, with whose elements an organization is interdependent, transmitted to that organization? It is generally accepted that environments affect organizations, but how that happens is not made explicit. Pfeffer and Salancik suggest that one means is executive succession. That is, the removal of executives and their replacement by others. Through this the environment influences the political processes within organizations from which action emerges.

There are three causal steps in Pfeffer and Salancik's argument about executive succession. To begin with, changes in whichever sectors of the environment are uncertain and which are less so mould the pattern of power in an organization. This occurs as posited by the 'strategic contingencies theory of intraorganizational power' formulated by Hickson, Hinings and their colleagues (see under Pugh and the Aston Group p. 9). According to this theory, those sections or sub-units of organizations most able to cope with what is uncertain to an organization (e.g. a marketing department smoothing out erratic fluctuations in orders by shrewdly timed advertising, or a maintenance department keeping production flowing by skilled attention to breakdowns) gain power, subject to two conditions. They must be non-substitutable (no one else can do what they do) and central (many others in the organization are affected by what they do, and the organization's main outputs would be affected immediately if they ceased to do it).

The resulting distribution of power then affects the choice of top personnel. As Pfeffer and Salancik put it, 'We view administrative succession as a political process of contested capability, where the contest is resolved by sub-unit power.' There is a tendency to blame top management for difficulties, the counterpart to their own tendency to take credit for successes in a world over which they have limited control. So they tend to be removed if things go badly, and who is removed and who replaces them follows the perceptions of the powerful of who can best cope with the perceived uncertain dependencies.

The third step in the argument is that executives and administrators once appointed can and do influence the main directive decisions. Although their control over their world is limited, they do have sufficient to shape decisions. They take part in what Child has called 'strategic choice' (see under Pugh and the Aston Group, p. 12) which delineates the intended future course of their organization. They 'enact' an environment, acting according to how they see it, and trying to change it to their organization's advantage. Further, changes in top personnel permit movement between organizations and this can be a tacit means of coordination. The managers of one know the managers in another.

Top managements are especially concerned with scanning the environment to find out what is happening and what may happen, and with loosening dependencies so that the organization does not become too dependent on any one or few others, and with managing conflicting external demands. It has been fashionable to forecast that the environment they face will become more and more dispersed and turbulent, but Pfeffer and Salancik do not agree. They foresee 'an increasingly interconnected environment in which power is increasingly concentrated'. Though they write in terms of the American variant of the capitalist system, their resource dependence perspective generalizes beyond that.

BIBLIOGRAPHY

PFEFFER, J., and SALANCIK, G. R., *The External Control of Organizations: a Resource Dependence Perspective*, Harper & Row, 1978.

Raymond E. Miles and Charles C. Snow

Raymond Miles and Charles Snow are both professors in American Business Schools. Miles is Professor of Business Administration at the University of California, Berkeley. He has studied and advised a wide variety of organizations in the public and private sectors. Snow is Professor of Organizational Behaviour at Pennsylvania State University.

Miles and Snow ask how and why organizations differ in strategy, in structure, in technology and in administration. Why do some offer a broad range of products or services and others a narrower range? Why are some structured around functional specialisms and others around product lines or services? Why are some more centralized, others more decentralized? For Miles and Snow the answers can be found with Thompson (see p. 51) in what he termed the alignment of organization with environment.

To align organization and environment successfully, management has to solve three problems, and solve them continuously. They are the entrepreneurial, engineering, and administrative problems. The *entrepreneurial problem* is to choose a general market domain, or field of operation, in which the organization can be viable, to specify the precise target market, and decide on the right products or services for it. Solving this problem, however, requires also solving the *engineering problem*, taking the word engineering in a wide sense. Ways have to be found of making the products or offering the services. There must be appropriate technologies. Then the *administrative problem* is to organize and manage the work.

The aim should be an effective *adaptive cycle*. This means that the entrepreneurial, engineering and administrative problems are tackled in coherent, mutually complementary ways which enable the organization as a whole to survive.

In studies of a variety of kinds of organization Miles and Snow find four types of *adaptation strategy*, pursued by organizations which they name Defenders, Prospectors, Analysers and Reactors. Defenders and Prospectors are at opposite ends of the continuum of possible strategies. Analysers are somewhere in between with some of the features of both. Each of these three types has its own typical solutions to the entrepreneurial, engineering and administrative problems. Reactors are different again. They seem unable to consistently pursue any of the other three types of strategy, reacting to events in an inconsistent way.

The first type, the *Defenders*, chooses to solve the entrepreneurial problem by aiming at a narrow and stable domain. They set themselves to sustain a prominent position in a narrow market segment, competing on either or both of quality and price to keep a particular clientele satisfied. They grow cautiously, step by step, by deeper penetration of this limited market. They reap the benefits of familiarity with it and with what they are doing, but tend to miss new developments because their managerial personnel have a restricted range of external contacts. There is a risk of them being caught by a major market shift to which they cannot adapt quickly enough.

Defenders are inclined to concentrate mostly on their engineering problem. Solving it is the key to their success. They succeed by being cost-efficient in doing what they know how to do well. They concentrate on improving quality control, production scheduling, materials handling and inventory control, distribution, and the like. They buffer their core technology from external disturbance, as Thompson would put it, by carrying stocks of supplies and of products so that though there may be ups and downs in stocks, the production work itself can proceed steadily. Buffering may be helped through vertical integration with other organizations (i.e. by mutual ownership or contracts which ensure supplies and orders). However, while a Defender may work efficiently, here again there is a risk. It may be a long time before the investment in technology pays off.

Defender-type solutions to the entrepreneurial and administrative problems lead to a typical administrative solution. Efficient supplying of a limited clientele requires relatively centralized control. Instructions flow down from the top, and reports and explanations flow upwards, via a 'long-looped vertical information system'. There is a central array of specialist departments, such as accounting, sales and personnel, administering a range of formalized documented procedures such as budget returns, work schedules, and stock listings. Together with the Chief Executive, the crucial finance and production functions dominate the centralized system. As always there are risks. While the system is orderly, novel opportunities may pass it by.

A Defender strategy has been pursued successfully by a food company in North California described by Miles and Snow. It has stayed within a speciality market for dried fruits and fruit juices. Beginning just by growing these, it met competition by extending into processing the fruit for consumption. This work has been mechanized, costs of growing fruit have been held down, and a small team specializes in improving quality. Control is centralized on the President and the heads of field operations, sales and finance, and higher than average wages ensure a stable labour force. The firm has a long-term coherence of entrepreneurial, engineering, and administrative solutions.

The second type, *Prospectors*, the opposite of the Defenders, aims to find and exploit new opportunities. They stress 'doing the right things' rather than 'doing things right' as Defenders do. They may value a reputation for innovation more than they value profitability. Solving the entrepreneurial problem this way requires keeping in touch with trends and events across a wide field of view. A variety of individuals and sections in the organization bring in news of current happenings, not necessarily only the more obvious ones such as the market research or research and development departments. Growth comes from new products or services and from new markets, rather than from deeper penetration of the same market as with a Defender. It is likely to occur in spurts as opportunities are successfully taken up, rather than gradually. The gain to Prospectors from being open to fresh possibilities has to be balanced against the risks: that they may not be fully efficient in any one activity, and may over-extend themselves by taking on too much without sufficient recompense.

Their enterprising approach to the entrepreneurial problem requires a flexible solution to the engineering problem, so they use a variety of technologies. They do many things at once and can switch between them. Each line of work can be built up or discontinued fairly readily. There has to be trial and error work on prototypes. The gain is a flexible workforce; the cost is the difficulties of coordinating such a diversity of differing activity.

These solutions to the entrepreneurial and engineering problems are accompanied by a typical solution to the administrative problem. In the case of a Prospector, the administrative problem is how to facilitate all this activity, rather than how to control it. How can resources be deployed effectively without impeding the work by imposing inappropriately rigid central control? The answer is to plan broadly but not in detail. Skilled personnel can be relied on to know their jobs without detailed overseeing from the top. Small groups are gathered in project teams or task forces to work on new initiatives, and these, together with easy lateral contact between departments, create 'short horizontal feedback loops'. In other words, lines of communication are comparatively short. People can communicate quickly with anyone they need to contact without having to go to the top first. The structure is comparatively decentralized, and the marketing and the research and development functions are more influential than in a Defender. The advantage of this administrative solution overall is that it can respond rapidly to change, but inevitably there are risks. Some attempts to launch new products or services will be wasteful failures, costly both in capital and in the time of highly paid personnel.

Miles and Snow exemplify the Prospector strategy by the success of an electronics corporation. This huge enterprise, with 30,000 employees, makes and sells an extensive range of equipment including small computers, calculators, electric meters and electrical testing equipment. Its entrepreneurial strategy is to keep one step ahead. There are frequent launches of new products with novelty value which fetch high prices. By the time prices fall, either the firm can manufacture cheaply just as its competitors have learned to, or another new launch is ready. Teams of scientists and engineers work on new possibilities, backed by the powerful marketing function whenever a new product is ready. The tendency is to create relatively autonomous divisions in each new product area. The company has a widely active and decentralized entrepreneurial, engineering and administrative pattern, quite different to the focused centralized Defender pattern.

Analysers attempt to achieve some of the strengths of both Defenders and Prospectors. They try to balance the minimizing of risk and the maximizing of profits. Their solution to the entrepreneurial problem is a mixture of stable and changing products and markets. Their stable activities generate earnings sufficient to enable them to move into innovative areas already opened up by Prospectors who have taken the early risks. The Analyser is a follower of change, not an initiator.

Since Analysers have something of both the Defender and of the Prospector entrepreneurial solutions, they are likely to have something of both engineering solutions. They are likely to have a dual technical core. That is, some of the work will be stable and routinized, while some will be shifting as new products are accepted and put into production quickly without the prolonged experimentation that a Prospector has to do. This combined solution to the engineering problem demands a corresponding dual administrative solution. There is both detailed control of stable lines and broad planning of innovations. Both production and marketing are influential, but so too, uniquely, are the personnel in applied research, since they are critical to getting new products into production. There are both central functional specialisms and also autonomous self-contained product groups.

Among examples of Analysers, Miles and Snow cite a medium-sized American general hospital. After many years of stability as a Defender, it underwent a series of changes. These were intended to enable it to offer new services already offered by more innovative hospitals while still sustaining its traditional, relatively conventional, patient care. This change in solution to its entrepreneurial problem required it to move toward Prospector-type engineering and administrative solutions. While retaining existing medical technology, it acquired modern diagnostic equipment and the technical and medical staff to go with it. Administratively, its previous unitary structure was broken down into three semi-autonomous divisions, one of which contained all the new diagnostic services and clinics. It succeeded in following others into this kind of work, and in attracting a fresh range of lower-income patients, while keeping its established higher-income clientele.

Defenders, Prospectors and Analysers have viable strategies, but *Reactors* do not. They are an unstable form. They fail to achieve or hold to an appropriate defending, prospecting or analysing strategy. As a result, they are liable merely to react to change and to do so in ways that are both inconsistent and inappropriate, so they perform poorly. This makes them hesitant over what to do next. There are many possible reasons for this condition. Miles and Snow give examples of three. Perhaps the strategy is not 'articulated', so that managers are not fully aware of it, as sometimes happens when a strategy pursued successfully by a firm's founder dies with him and leaves the managers in disarray, not knowing what to do without him. Perhaps, even though there is a recognized strategy, the technology and the structure do not fit it, as when a publishing firm aspired to an Analyser strategy but could not separate its stable lines of work which needed careful central control, from its changing lines which needed scope for trial and error. Possibly, both strategy and structure persist inappositely, as when a foods firm clung on to its long-established Defender strategy and structure even though declining profitability in a changing market pointed to the need for change.

Miles and Snow look beyond this typology of strategies to conjecture over signs of the future emergence of yet another type. This they call the *Market-Matrix* form of organization. It would 'pursue mixed strategies with mixed structures'. Some have moved towards it, from among recent kinds of organizations, such as conglomerates, multi-national corporations, aerospace firms and certain educational institutions. They have matrix sections where lines of authority deliberately intersect or double up (e.g. where a department head also has responsibility for a major innovative project). A further step is then to expect such a project manager to bargain internally, market-fashion, for resources and for skilled personnel, the personnel having to be 'purchased' from existing departments. So a new form may be arising which is fitted to complex tasks.

Miles and Snow intend their typology to help managers determine what kind of strategy to pursue. They present a Diagnostic Checklist of questions on an organization's present and potential strategies to use for this purpose.

BIBLIOGRAPHY

MILES, R. E., and SNOW, C. C., *Organizational Strategy, Structure and Process*, McGraw-Hill, 1978.

MILES, R. E., and SNOW, C. C., 'Fit, Failure and the Hall of Fame', *California Management Review*, 1984, 26, 10–28; reprinted in D. S. Pugh (ed.), *Organization Theory*, Penguin, 1990.

Michael T. Hannan and John Freeman

Michael Hannan and John Freeman are both social scientists at Cornell University. After a period at Stanford University, Hannan moved to Cornell where his co-author Freeman had been for many years. Hannan is Scarborough Professor of Social Sciences. Freeman is Professor of Behavioural and Organizational Sciences and editor of the journal *Administrative Science Quarterly*.

It has been the shared aim of Hannan and Freeman to lift the view taken of organizations to a wider perspective. They have done this by looking at organizations much as a bioecologist or naturalist looks at animal life. They see populations of organizations surviving or thriving or declining in particular environments, just as populations of, say, rabbits survive or thrive in a particular ecological situation but die out in another. Just as the understanding of wildlife has been enhanced by the study of ecology, so can the understanding of organizations be enhanced. The wider ecological perspective goes beyond the problems each organization alone has in coping with the environment, to see an organization as one of a population which coexists with or competes with other populations of organizations. The environment of each consists mainly of other organizations, so the existence of each is bound up with that of its own kind and of other kinds. Hence the *population ecology of organizations*.

Societies engage in many kinds of activities, and there are many different kinds of service and manufacturing organizations to do these activities. Why so many, and why does the number of different kinds rise and fall? This question is the same as 'Why are there so many species of animals?', and for both organizations and animals, population ecology explains the replacement of outmoded forms by new forms.

Indeed, the ability of a whole society to keep up with change depends upon the development of new forms of organization. If a society contains many differing forms of organization, then there is a good chance that one or more of these may fit some new circumstances which arise and these new circumstances can then be taken advantage of quickly. If there are comparatively few forms of organization in a society, it has to adapt to change by modifying one or more of these or by creating a new form, and this takes longer. So a society that already has, among its hospitals, some which specialize in advanced surgery can readily add on heart transplant techniques; if it has only a uniform range of general hospitals dealing with the most common and cheaply treated ailments it has more difficulty in doing so.

This view assumes that populations of organizations evolve much as populations of biological species evolve. Those that fit their situation survive and thrive and those that do not die out. This is a 'Darwinian evolutionary position'. It argues that change takes place more by the growth of new forms of organization than by the intended reform of existing ones. Many theorists have pointed out that change in an organization is largely uncontrolled. Though its management may well believe that they are making changes according to plan, what happens is more haphazard than that. Differing views, unreliable information, and unforeseen eventualities make it uncertain whether they will get what they want, even if they know what they want (March p. 123, Thompson p. 51). Therefore a Darwinian explanation that some forms fit the situation and prosper while others fail to fit and so decline, is more tenable than supposing managements succeed in deliberately redesigning existing organizations to bring them up to date. Burns (p. 41) described an example of this. Several well-established firms in Britain were unable to change sufficiently to move into the new field of electronics, though offered every encouragement to do so. Their form of organization was too fixed.

The evolution of populations of organizations is not necessarily a steady process. It is more likely that there are periods of rapid change as new forms are tried out, interspersed with comparative stability during which existing forms persist. This would match contemporary views of biological evolution which regard it as 'punctuated equilibria' – long periods of comparatively balanced stability broken by shorter spasms of change. American labour unions did not grow steadily in number. There were spurts of activity at the end of the nineteenth century, again after the first World War, and again in the 1930s, when many new unions were founded. In between these peaks relatively few new ones appeared.

Hannan and Freeman concentrate on the density within each population (i.e. the number of organizations of a particular form). The density of a population is determined by how many organizations come and go. In other words, it is determined by how many are newly founded or come in from elsewhere, and by how many cease to exist or leave to do something different.

There are limits to density. Each *niche* in an environment can support a population density up to the limit of the *carrying capacity* of that niche. When the resources of a niche are exhausted, density can rise no further. That is, when competition for money and supplies and customers, or whatever else is needed, reaches an unsustainable level, some organizations will be squeezed out. This is analogous to what happens to wildlife when numbers become too great. Those who study wildlife regard a niche for insects or animals as 'the set of environmental conditions within which a population can grow or at least sustain its numbers'. In the niches inhabited by organizations, too, there is only room for so many.

Given these assumptions about organizations, Hannan and Freeman consider first how fast new organizations in a population are founded (the rate of *founding*), and then how fast they die out (the rate of *disbanding*). Consider founding. The fact that there are a growing number of a particular form of organization relative to the capacity of an environmental niche does not necessarily stop new entrants. Indeed, Hannan and Freeman contend that at first the rate of founding increases as density increases. The more there are, the more new ones attempt to get in. This is because a high density means more of that form of organization are around so people become accustomed to them. Their existence is less likely to be questioned. They acquire greater legitimacy, as labour unions did after precarious early years when their right to exist was challenged. Further, the rate of new foundings may increase as total numbers grow also because there are more and more people who have experience of how to set up such an organization. The know-how is available. But there comes that level at which the niche can take no more, the level at which some are being squeezed out, and then launching new ones is no longer attractive. Then the rate of founding falls. So Hannan and Freeman argue that as the total number of organizations of a given form grows, first there are more new entrants and then there are less, because 'density increases legitimacy at a decreasing rate' but 'increases competition at an increasing rate'. If foundings are plotted against density, there should be a u-shaped curve.

This is shown in the United States in populations of organizations as different as labour unions, newspapers and semiconductor electronics firms. The history of unions and newspapers shows the pattern of first a rise and then a fall in foundings, while total numbers (density) increase, the pattern originating far back in the nineteenth century. Electronics is a much more recent and volatile population of the mid twentieth century. Here density increased rapidly as firms rushed to join this new industry, and so competition forced down the rate of entry to the industry much more quickly than was the case with the unions and newspapers.

Disbanding, or 'mortality', is held to be the other way around. As the total number of organizations in a population grows, there are first less disbandings and then more. Of course, the number of disbandings, the 'fatalities' in a population through closures or withdrawals from their field, may actually start quite high for the same reason that foundings start low, because legitimacy and know-how are hard to get when few of a kind exist. But the rate of disbandings soon drops as survival becomes easier, and so there are fewer and fewer disbandings, and more and more survivors. Once again, however, when density reaches a level where the niche can support no more, the trend changes. It swings round from a falling rate of disbandings to an increasing rate. Competition forces organizations out, and the number of disbandings begins to rise and may go on rising as long as density goes on rising.

Plotting disbandings against density should produce an *inverted* u-shape. So indeed it did for the unions, newspapers and electronics populations. The rate of disbanding dropped sharply for all three as their total numbers increased, and then rose again under the pressure of competition. But the force of competitive pressure appeared to differ. It seemed weakest for newspapers, stronger for electronics firms, and strongest for unions, which squeezed each other out more and more once the critical density of union population was reached. The existence of a large number of craft unions, with members from the same occupations in many industries, seemed detrimental especially to industrial unions with members from many occupations in a single industry, for as the density of craft unions rose so too did the disbanding of industrial unions.

Disbandings are also influenced by age and size of organization. Hannan and Freeman do not agree with assertions that modern organizations are (or should be) in a state of constant flux and innovation. As they see it, organizations persist because of their reliability in outputs of goods and services, and their accountability for the use of resources, each of which increase with institutionalization and stability. So the stability of age improves the chances of survival, despite the inertia that ageing can bring. There are fewer disbandings in populations of older organizations. Older unions and older firms are less likely to close down or merge than are younger ones.

Growth, too, improves the chances. Although bigger organizations similarly may have greater structural inertia, they have the resources to withstand shocks from their environments. 'Small organizations are more likely than large ones to attempt change, but are more likely to disappear in the process.'

Within populations, sub-populations are found to respond differently to different environmental niche conditions. Thus among both restaurants and semiconductor firms, generalists (with a relatively wide range of services or products) are found to do better under variable conditions.

Specialists (with a narrower range) do better in stable cyclical conditions, called coarse-grained environments (where there are known long-term business cycles).

As applied to organizations by Hannan and Freeman, population ecology theory questions the usefulness of the efforts commonly made to reform existing organizations as managements attempt to keep up with change. It implies that populations or organizations change more effectively by selection and replacement than by adaptation. To effect change, start a new organization

Here population ecology theory becomes practical, for potentially it can show whether 'the dice are loaded for or against a particular way of doing business'. There is no best form of organization, but many forms for many niches.

BIBLIOGRAPHY

HANNAN, M. T., and FREEMAN, J., *Organizational Ecology*, Harvard University Press, 1988.

Oliver E. Williamson

Oliver Williamson, an American economist, began his working life as a project engineer in US government service, but soon moved into academic life taking degrees at the universities of Stanford and Carnegie-Mellon. His career took him through leading American universities to become, in 1983, Tweedy Professor of Economics of Law and Organization at Yale University.

Williamson probes beneath the usual questions about what organizations are like and how their members behave to ask why they are there at all. Why organizations? His answer is because they lower the cost of transactions. He sees society as a network of transactions – contracts in the widest sense of that term – and suggests that a 'transactional paradigm' will yield the reasons for organizations. These reasons are not size – that is, the economies of scale which have been supposed to explain large organizations – nor large-scale technologies, but the information cost of transactions. Size and technology are important not in themselves but because of the demands they make for information.

Each of the multitude of recurrent transactions which take place in a society can be conducted either in a market or within an organization. Which mode of transacting is used depends upon the information available and the costs to the transacting parties of adding to that information should they require more. So as the requirements for information change, transactions may be conducted more in markets, or more and more within organizations. The trend has been for more transactions to be gathered within the boundaries of organizations, and Williamson's discussion is primarily about change in that direction. That is because he has been concerned mainly with societies moving that way, but if the starting point were a society in which central planning and non-market transactions predominated, the analysis could as appropriately deal with the shifting of transactions from within organizations out to markets. Analysis of transaction costs can answer 'why not organizations?' as well as 'why organizations?'

Williamson's point of view joins market economics to organization theory in a form of institutional economics. He looks forward to the possibility that measures of market structure will eventually combine with measures of the internal structure of organizations (see Derek Pugh and the Aston Group, p. 9).

Markets and *hierarchies* are alternatives for conducting transactions. So transactions are brought within the hierarchical structures of organizations when the market mode is no longer efficient. For example, mergers or takeovers bring into a single organization contracting parties whose transactions will then be regulated by the internal rules of a hierarchy and not by the rules of a market. Or organizations are set up to transact within themselves business that might alternatively have been done by separate parties contracting between themselves in market terms.

Which mode is adopted depends upon the degree of *information impactedness*. This exists when the 'true underlying circumstances' of a transaction are known to one or more parties but not to others. Where there is less than complete trust between the parties, those who lack information could only obtain parity by incurring costs, which may be high, even prohibitive. Thus a buyer who is offered supplies may be unsure whether the quality will be what is required, whether delivery is likely to be on time, or how far the proposed price is more than need be paid. This may be because no one, not even the seller, has adequate information on these matters; or it may be that even if information is available, the buyer cannot trust it because the seller will have interpreted it to favour the selling vantage point.

A market is the most efficacious mode of conducting transactions when all necessary information is conveyed between parties by a price, and this single item of information is sufficient. Transactions are better brought within a hierarchy when much more must be known, much less is certain, and there may be 'quasi-moral' elements, for the hierarchy brings the inadequately informed parties to a transaction together under some degree of control.

Transactions will be shifted out of a market and into the hierarchy of a firm, or other form of organization, when information impactedness is high, that is when the uncertainties and distrust inherent in transactions become too great for prices to be acceptably determined. At this point the advantages of hierarchy become the greater. First, it extends the bounds on rationality. Though the rationalities of each of the parties within an organization are still restricted, specialization enables each to deal with a part of the overall problem that is small enough to be comprehended, the results of the work of them all being brought together by specialized decision makers at the apex. More information is exchanged or can be required to be handed over. Common numbering and coding systems and occupational jargon cut down communication costs. Second, sub-sections of an organization can each attend to a given aspect of the uncertainty-complexity of a situation so making manageable a problem which would in total be too uncertain-complex. Aspects can be attended to as the situation unfolds, rather than all at once, and decisions which might otherwise be too complex can be split down into smaller sequential steps (see Lindblom, p. 128). Third, a hierarchy curbs opportunism. Pay, promotion, and control techniques ensure that the parties work in some degree towards common goals. Confidence may not be complete but it is greater. Parties cannot use their gains entirely for their own ends, and what they do can be more effectively checked and audited. Should disputes arise, superior hierarchical levels can decide them. Fourth, where there are small numbers, a situation which opportunistic parties are inclined to take advantage of, the hierarchy can overrule bargaining.

In general then, hierarchy more nearly approaches parity of information, and in particular provides for quasi-moral and reciprocal obligations over and above strictly economic ones.

What then stops hierarchies taking over more and more transactions indefinitely? The limits begin to appear as firms grow larger and as vertical integration between firms extends. Costs then rise to a level at which the marginal costs of administering the incremental transaction begin to exceed those of completing transactions through a market. The goals of groups or sub-sections within an organization start to outweigh the common aims, the proliferation of specialists in control systems to combat this tendency becomes more and more expensive, sunk costs encourage the persistence of existing ways of doing things even if they would not now be done that way, were they to be started afresh, and communication is increasingly distorted. Leaders become more distant from those they lead – 'bureaucratic insularity' – and cooperation between those at lower levels becomes perfunctory rather than wholehearted. Coordination and common purpose lapse.

These costs rise in the unitary structure of hierarchy (called U-form), when the top management of the single large organization tries to control transactions within it. The U-form is therefore a vanishing breed among large US corporations, although the Reynolds Metal Company and the Quaker Oats Company retained this form right throughout the 1960s. Organizational transaction costs can be relatively reduced by the adoption of a multi-divisional structure (called M-form) as in the examples described by Chandler (see p. 27) of Du Pont, General Motors, Standard Oil of New Jersey and Sears Roebuck, who changed to the M-form in the twenties and thirties. To be effective, this form of organization requires a general overall management which concentrates on monitoring the performance of the constituent divisions and on strategic planning. Management can use the multi-divisional structure as a miniature capital market in which funds are moved into the most profitable uses more effectively than by the external capital market, because internally there is more complete information about the firm than parties in the external capital market have about comparative investment opportunities.

But if general management gets involved in the day-to-day operation of the divisions, then information costs will be again forced up, in what is called the 'corrupted M-form'. One large corporation is quoted as attempting to move from the corrupted M-form by releasing a total of 5,000 non-production personnel. It also reduced corporate staff – people not reporting to profit centres – by over 1,300, down to a new total of 132. The aim was to decentralize into true profit centres in which each divisional manager's performance could be accurately evaluated without the allocation of heavy corporate overheads.

If the change from the corrupted M-form cannot be achieved and the information costs remain high, then market transactions will become more attractive. For ultimately it is the relative cost of overcoming information impactedness that determines whether the transactions in a society are conducted through markets or within organizations.

BIBLIOGRAPHY

WILLIAMSON, O. E., *Markets and Hierarchies: Analysis and Antitrust Implications*, Free Press, 1975.

WILLIAMSON, O. E., *Economic Organization*, Wheatsheaf Books, 1986.

Geert Hofstede

Geert Hofstede is a social psychologist who is currently Professor of Organizational Anthropology and International Management at the University of Limburg, the Netherlands, and Director of the Institute for Research on Inter-Cultural Cooperation there. In the early 1970s he and his colleagues carried out a major systematic study of work-related attitudes based on two questionnaire surveys, which produced a total of over 116,000 questionnaires from over seventy countries around the world – making it by far the largest organizationally-based study ever to have been carried out.

Those respondents whose replies were used by Hofstede for research purposes were all sales and service employees of subsidiaries of IBM – a U S based multinational corporation which operates in most countries in the world. Within the sales and service function all types of employees were surveyed – sales clerks, professional engineers, top managers, etc. – using the language of each country. A total of twenty different language versions of the questionnaire had to be made. The IBM employees represented well matched sub-sets from each country: same company, job and education but different nationalities. National cultural differences found within the company, therefore, are likely to be a conservative estimate of those existing within the countries at large. The survey was repeated after four years with stable results, underlining the cultural nature of the differences found.

Hofstede identifies four basic dimensions of the differences between national cultures based on the forty larger subsidiaries on which the first analyses were made. Each of the national cultures can be positioned from high to low on each of the four scales, and thus has a distinctive cultural profile. The four dimensions are:

1. Power–distance
2. Uncertainty–avoidance
3. Individualism
4. Masculinity

The power–distance dimension is concerned with how far the culture encourages superiors to exert power. In a high power–distance culture (e.g. France, India) that is what being a boss means. Inequality is accepted: 'a place for everyone and everyone in his place'. So employees are frequently afraid to express disagreement with their bosses, and prefer to work for managers who take the decisions – and the responsibility – and then simply tell them what to do.

In a low power–distance culture (e.g. Austria, Israel) superiors and subordinates consider each other to be colleagues and both believe that inequalities in society should be minimized. So those in power should try to look less powerful than they are. Employees are seldom afraid to disagree, and expect to be consulted before decisions are made.

The uncertainty–avoidance dimension is the ease with which the culture copes with novelty. In strong uncertainty–avoidance cultures (e.g. Japan, Greece) people feel the need for clarity and order. They feel threatened by uncertain situations, and higher anxiety and stress are experienced. This is combated by hard work, career stability and intolerance of deviancy. Thus employees believe that company rules should not be broken – even when it is shown to be in the company's best interest – and look forward to continue working with the firm until they retire.

In a weak uncertainty–avoidance culture (e.g. Denmark, Hong Kong) the uncertainty inherent in life is more easily accepted and each day is taken as it comes. A very pragmatic view is taken about keeping or changing those rules which are in existence, and employees expect to be working for the firm for much shorter periods.

The individualism dimension focuses on the degree to which the culture encourages individual as opposed to collectivist, group-centred concerns. In an individualist culture (e.g. USA, Britain) the emphasis is on personal initiative and achievement, and everyone has the right to a private life and opinion. By contrast, a collectivist culture (e.g. Iran, Peru) is characterized by a tighter social framework, where people are members of extended families or clans which protect them in exchange for loyalty. The emphasis is on belonging and the aim is to be a good member – whereas in the individualist culture the ideal is to be a good leader. Collectivist involvement in the work organization is a moral one and requires full commitment.

The masculinity dimension highlights 'masculine' cultures (e.g. Australia, Italy) where performance is what counts; money and material standards are important, ambition is the driving force. Big and fast are beautiful; 'machismo' is sexy. In contrast, in 'feminine' cultures (e.g. the Netherlands, Sweden) it is the quality of life that matters: people and the environment are important, service provides the motivation, small is beautiful and unisex is attractive. The expected relationship of men to women differs considerably along this dimension. In 'masculine' cultures the sex roles are clearly differentiated. Men should be assertive, dominating; women should be caring, nurturing. In 'feminine' cultures the sex roles are more flexible, and there is a belief in equality between the sexes. It is not 'unmasculine' for a man to take a caring role, for example.

Equipped with measurements which locate the forty cultures along the four dimensions, Hofstede then offers a set of cultural maps of the world. Two points should be remembered in interpreting the results. The first is that countries are located along the whole of each of the four dimensions, not only at the extremes. So cultures are not only masculine like Italy or feminine like Sweden; there are also many countries in between: Belgium exactly in the centre; Britain on the masculine side, France on the feminine one.

The second point to remember is that the position of a culture along a dimension is based on the averages for all the respondents in that particular country. Characterizing a national work culture does not mean that every person in the nation has all the characteristics ascribed to that culture – there are bound to be many individual variations. There are, for example, many Japanese who are risk takers and many from Hong Kong who avoid uncertainty; many Indians with low power–distance values and many Israelis with high power–distance attitudes. What these scales are doing is describing the common values of the central core of the culture which come about through the 'collective mental programming' of a number of people (a tribe, a nation or a national minority) who are conditioned by the same life experience and the same education. Although this will not make everybody the same, a country's nationals do share a cultural character – which is indeed more clearly visible to foreigners than to themselves.

The table (opposite) gives a classification of the nations grouped by cultural similarity according to the statistical technique of cluster analysis. They fall into eight areas. Since a culture's work-related values are so distinctive and different, it is to be expected that its organizational processes and behaviour would be so too. Hofstede argues very strongly that we should not expect the same conceptions and prescriptions about management to be appropriate for all culture areas.

Hofstede illustrates this cultural approach by examining the way in which a specific management practice has operated in several cultures. Management by Objectives (MbO) as advocated by Peter Drucker (see p. 98) started in the United States and has had most success there, particularly in situations where the manager's results can be objectively measured.

Why is this so? MbO requires that:

1. subordinates are sufficiently independent to negotiate meaningfully with the boss (i.e. low power–distance).

Country clusters and their characteristics

I: More developed Latin	II: Less developed Latin
high power–distance high uncertainty–avoidance medium to high individualism medium masculinity	high power–distance high uncertainty–avoidance low individualism whole range on masculinity
BELGIUM FRANCE ARGENTINA BRAZIL SPAIN (ITALY)	COLOMBIA MEXICO VENEZUELA CHILE PERU PORTUGAL

III: More developed Asian	IV: Less developed Asian	V: Near Eastern
medium power–distance high uncertainty–avoidance medium individualism high masculinity	high power–distance low to medium uncertainty–avoidance low individualism medium masculinity	high power–distance high uncertainty–avoidance low individualism medium masculinity
JAPAN	PAKISTAN TAIWAN THAILAND HONG KONG INDIA PHILIPPINES SINGAPORE	GREECE IRAN TURKEY (YUGOSLAVIA)

VI: Germanic	VII: Anglo	VIII: Nordic
low power–distance medium to high uncertainty–avoidance medium individualism medium to high masculinity	low to medium power–distance low to medium uncertainty–avoidance high individualism high masculinity	low power–distance low to medium uncertainty–avoidance medium to high individualism low masculinity
AUSTRIA ISRAEL GERMANY SWITZERLAND	AUSTRALIA CANADA BRITAIN IRELAND NEW ZEALAND USA (SOUTH AFRICA)	DENMARK FINLAND NETHERLANDS NORWAY SWEDEN

(from Hofstede, 1980.)

2. both are willing to take some risks – the boss in delegating power, the subordinate in accepting responsibility (i.e. low uncertainty – avoidance).
3. the subordinate is personally willing to 'have a go' and make a mark (i.e. high individualism).
4. both regard performance and results achieved as important (i.e. high masculinity).

This is the Anglo work-culture pattern as the table shows.

But how would MbO work out in other culture areas? For example the Germanic culture area has low power–distance which fits, as does the results orientation of high masculinity. However the Germanic group is high on uncertainty–avoidance which would work against the risk taking and ambiguity involved in the Anglo process. But the idea of replacing the arbitrary authority of the boss with the impersonal authority of mutually agreed objectives fits well in this culture. This is, indeed, the way MbO has developed in Germany, emphasizing the need to develop procedures of a more participative kind. The German name for MbO is 'Management by Joint Goal Setting' and elaborate formal systems have been developed. There is also great stress on team objectives (as opposed to the individual emphasis in the Anglo culture) and this fits in with the lower individualism of this culture area.

The More developed Latin group, as represented by France, has high power–distance and high uncertainty–avoidance – completely the opposite to the Anglo group – so MbO is bound to encounter difficulties there. It did gain some popularity in France for a time, but it was not sustained. The problem was that in a high power–distance culture attempting to substitute the personal authority of the boss by self-monitored objectives is bound to generate anxiety. The boss does not delegate easily and will not stop short-circuiting intermediate hierarchical levels if necessary – and subordinates will expect this to happen and to be told what to do. And in a high uncertainty–avoidance culture, anxiety will be alleviated by sticking to the old ways.

Cultural differences, then, have an important impact on how organizations function, and manufacturing cars or treating the sick will call for different structures and processes in France or Japan or Britain. So it is important even for international organizations to have a dominant national culture to fall back on (e.g. as the American or Japanese multinationals). Organizations without a home culture, in which the key decision-makers can come from any country (e.g. UNESCO, the EEC Commission) find it very difficult to function effectively because of this lack. It is less of a problem for the political part of such organizations, since negotiation between representatives is their task. But for the administrative apparatus, where the members represent not their countries but the organization as a whole, it is crippling – and most such 'cultureless' organizations are inefficient and wasteful.

BIBLIOGRAPHY

HOFSTEDE, G., *Culture's Consequences*, Sage Publications, 1980.

HOFSTEDE, G., 'Motivation, Leadership and Organization: Do American Theories Apply Abroad?' *Organizational Dynamics* (Summer 1980), 42–63; reprinted in D. S. Pugh (ed.), *Organization Theory*, Penguin, 1990.

3 The Management of Organizations

To manage is to forecast and plan, to organize, to command, to coordinate and to control.
HENRI FAYOL

Scientific management will mean, for the employers and the workmen who adopt it, the elimination of almost all causes for dispute and disagreement between them.
FREDERICK W. TAYLOR

It [modern management] was to ensure that as a craft declined the worker would sink to the level of general and undifferentiated labour power, adaptable to a large range of simple tasks, while as science grew, it would be concentrated in the hands of management.
HARRY BRAVERMAN

The needs of large-scale organization have to be satisfied by common people achieving uncommon performance.
PETER F. DRUCKER

Excellent companies were, above all, 'brilliant on the basics'.
THOMAS J. PETERS and ROBERT H. WATERMAN

A 'Z' company can balance social relationships with productivity because the two relate closely anyway: a society and an economy represent two facets of one nation.
WILLIAM OUCHI

The degree to which the opportunity to use power effectively is granted or withheld from individuals is one operative difference between those companies which stagnate and those which innovate.
ROSABETH MOSS KANTER

Organizations with different structures, functioning in different environments, have to be managed. As long as there is management there will be the problem of how to manage better. In one sense, attempts at answers to the problem will be as numerous as there are managers, for each will bring an individual approach to the task. None the less, at any one time there is enough in common for there to be broad similarities in what is thought and what is taught on this issue. The writers in this section have each sought to improve the understanding of administration and its practice. They have looked for the ingredients of a better management.

Henri Fayol puts forward a classic analysis of the management task, based on his long practical experience of doing the job, and the personal insights he gained. F. W. Taylor's name is synonymous with the term 'scientific management'. His extremely influential ideas made him a controversial figure in his own day and have remained a subject for much argument. Harry Braverman, from a Marxist perspective, mounts a critique on the degradation which Taylor's ideas bring to modern work.

Peter Drucker emphasizes the necessity of 'management by objectives' if high performance is to be achieved. Thomas Peters and Robert Waterman, in an influential analysis, report a set of eight attributes which characterize excellent firms, and propose that they should be widely adopted. William Ouchi asks what management lessons the West can learn from Japanese companies, and suggests adaptations which can be beneficially applied. Rosabeth Moss Kanter proposes ways in which organizations should be managed to draw more fully on the total human resources within them.

Henri Fayol

Henri Fayol (1841–1925) was a mining engineer by training. A Frenchman, he spent his working life with the French mining and metallurgical combine Commentry-Fourchamboult-Decazeville, first as an engineer but from his early thirties onwards in general management. From 1888 to 1918 he was Managing Director.

Fayol is among those who have achieved fame for ideas made known very late in life. He was in his seventies before he published them in a form which came to be widely read. He had written technical articles on mining engineering and a couple of preliminary papers on administration, but it was in 1916 that the *Bulletin de la Société de l'Industrie Minerale* printed Fayol's *Administration Industrielle et Générale – Prévoyance, Organisation, Commandement, Coordination, Contrôle.* He is also among those whose reputation rests on a single short publication still frequently reprinted as a book; his other writings are little known.

The English version appears as *General and Industrial Management*, translated by Constance Storrs and first issued in 1949. There has been some debate over this rendering of the title of the work, and in particular of expressing the French word '*administration*' by the term 'management'. It is argued that this could simply imply that Fayol is concerned only with industrial management, whereas his own preface claims that: 'Management plays a very important part in the government of undertakings; of all undertakings, large or small, industrial, commercial, political, religious or any other.' Indeed, in his last years he studied the problems of State public services and lectured at the *École Supérieure de la Guerre*. So it can be accepted that his intention was to initiate a theoretical analysis appropriate to a wide range of organizations.

Fayol suggests that: 'All activities to which industrial undertakings give rise can be divided into the following groups:

1. Technical activities (production, manufacture, adaptation).
2. Commercial activities (buying, selling, exchange).
3. Financial activities (search for and optimum use of capital).
4. Security activities (protection of property and persons).

5. Accounting activities (stocktaking, balance sheet, costs, statistics).
6. Managerial activities (planning, organization, command, coordination, control).

Be the undertaking simple or complex, big or small, these six groups of activities or essential functions are always present.'

Most of these six groups of activities will be present in most jobs, but in varying measure, with the managerial element in particular being greatest in senior jobs and least or absent in direct production or lower clerical tasks. Managerial activities are specially emphasized as being universal to organizations. But it is a commonplace to ask: What is management? Is it anything that can be identified and stand on its own, or is it a word, a label, that has no substance?

Fayol's answer was unique at the time. The core of his contribution is his definition of management as comprising five elements:

1. To forecast and plan (in the French, *prévoyance*): 'examining the future and drawing up the plan of action'.
2. To organize: 'building up the structure, material and human, of the undertaking'.
3. To command: 'maintaining activity among the personnel'.
4. To coordinate: 'binding together, unifying and harmonizing all activity and effort'.
5. To control: 'seeing that everything occurs in conformity with established rule and expressed command'.

For Fayol, managing means looking ahead, which makes the process of *forecasting and planning* a central business activity. Management must 'assess the future and make provision for it'. To function adequately a business organization needs a plan which has the characteristics of 'unity, continuity, flexibility and precision'. The problems of planning which management must overcome are: making sure that the objectives of each part of the organization are securely welded together (unity); using both short- and long-term forecasting (continuity); being able to adapt the plan in the light of changing circumstances (flexibility); and attempting to accurately predict courses of action (precision). The essence of planning is to allow the optimum use of resources. Interestingly, Fayol in 1916 argued the necessity of a national plan for France, to be produced by the government.

To *organize* is 'building up the structure, material and human, of the undertaking'. The task of management is to build up an organization which will allow the basic activities to be carried out in an optimal manner. Central to this is a structure in which plans are efficiently prepared and carried out. There must be unity of command and direction, clear definition of responsibilities, precise decision making backed up by an efficient system for selecting and training managers.

Fayol's third element comes logically after the first two. An organization must start with a plan, a definition of its goals. It then must produce an organization structure appropriate to the achievement of those goals. Third, the organization must be put in motion, which is *command*, maintaining activity among the personnel. Through an ability to command, the manager obtains the best possible performance from subordinates. This must be done through example, knowledge of the business, knowledge of the subordinates, continuous contact with staff, and by maintaining a broad view of the directing function. In this way the manager maintains a high level of activity by instilling a sense of mission.

Command refers to the relationship between a manager and the subordinates in the area of the immediate task. But organizations have a variety of tasks to perform, so *coordination* is necessary 'binding together, unifying and harmonizing all activity and effort'. Essentially this is making sure that one department's efforts are coincident with the efforts of other departments, and keeping all activities in perspective with regard to the overall aims of the organization. This can only be attained by a constant circulation of information and regular meetings of management.

Finally there is *control*, logically the final element which checks that the other four elements are in fact performing properly: 'seeing that everything occurs in conformity with established rule and expressed command.' To be effective, control must operate quickly and there must be a system of sanctions. The best way to ensure this is to separate all functions concerned with inspection from the operation departments whose work they inspect. Fayol believed in independent, impartial staff departments.

Fayol uses this classification to divide up his chapters on how to administer or manage. It is probable that when he wrote of *'une doctrine administrative'* he had in mind not only the above theory but the addition of experience to theoretical analysis to form a doctrine of good management. He summarizes the lessons of his own experience in a number of General Principles of Management. These are his own rules and he does not assume they are necessarily of universal application nor that they have any great permanence. None the less, most have become part of managerial know-how and many are regarded as fundamental tenets. Fayol outlines the following fourteen principles:

1. Division of work: specialization allows the individual to build up expertise and thereby be more productive.
2. Authority: the right to issue commands, along with which must go

the equivalent responsibility for its exercise.

3. Discipline: which is two-sided, for employees only obey orders if management play their part by providing good leadership.
4. Unity of command: in contrast to F. W. Taylor's functional authority (see p. 90), Fayol was quite clear that each worker should have only one boss with no other conflicting lines of command. On this issue history has favoured Fayol, for his principle has found most adherents among managers.
5. Unity of direction: people engaged in the same kind of activities must have the same objectives in a single plan.
6. Subordination of individual interest to general interest: management must see that the goals of the firm are always paramount.
7. Remuneration: payment is an important motivator although, by analysing a number of different possibilities, Fayol points out that there is no such thing as a perfect system.
8. Centralization or decentralization: again this is a matter of degree depending on the condition of the business and the quality of its personnel.
9. Scalar chain: a hierarchy is necessary for unity of direction but lateral communication is also fundamental as long as superiors know that such communication is taking place.
10. Order: both material order and social order are necessary. The former minimizes lost time and useless handling of materials. The latter is achieved through organization and selection.
11. Equity: in running a business, a 'combination of kindliness and justice' is needed in treating employees if equity is to be achieved.
12. Stability of tenure: this is essential due to the time and expense involved in training good management. Fayol believes that successful businesses tend to have more stable managerial personnel.
13. Initiative: allowing all personnel to show their initiative in some way is a source of strength for the organization even though it may well involve a sacrifice of 'personal vanity' on the part of many managers.
14. *Esprit de corps:* management must foster the morale of its employees and, to quote Fayol, 'real talent is needed to coordinate effort, encourage keenness, use each person's abilities, and reward each one's merit without arousing possible jealousies and disturbing harmonious relations'.

But Fayol's pride of place in this field is due not so much to his principles of how to manage, enduring though these are, as to his definition of what management is. He is the earliest known proponent of a theoretical analysis of managerial activities – an analysis which has withstood a half-century of critical discussion. There can have been few writers since who have not been influenced by it; and his five elements have provided a system of concepts with which managers may clarify their thinking about what it is they have to do.

BIBLIOGRAPHY

FAYOL, H., *General and Industrial Management*, Pitman, 1949. Translated by Constance Storrs from the original *Administration Industrielle et Générale*, 1916.

Frederick W. Taylor

Frederick Winslow Taylor (1856–1917) was an engineer by training. He joined the Midvale Steel Works as a labourer and rose rapidly to be foreman and later Chief Engineer. He was afterwards employed at the Bethlehem Steel Works, then became a consultant and devoted his time to the propagation of his ideas.

He first published his views on management in a paper entitled 'A piece rate system', read to the American Society of Mechanical Engineers in 1895. These views were expanded into a book *Shop Management* (1903) and further developed in *Principles of Scientific Management* (1911). As a result of labour troubles caused by the attempt to apply his principles in a government arsenal, a House of Representatives' Special Committee was set up in 1911 to investigate Taylor's system of shop management. (A full description of events at the arsenal is given in Aitken's case study.) In 1947, *Shop Management*, the *Principles*, and Taylor's Testimony to the Special Committee were collected together and published under the title of *Scientific Management*.

Taylor was the founder of the movement known as 'scientific management'. 'The principal object of management', he states, 'should be to secure the maximum prosperity for the employer, coupled with the maximum prosperity of each employee.' For the employer, 'maximum prosperity' means not just large profits in the short term but the development of all aspects of the enterprise to a state of permanent prosperity. For the employees 'maximum prosperity' means not just immediate higher wages, but their development so that they may perform efficiently in the highest grade of work for which their natural abilities fit them. The mutual interdependence of management and workers, and the necessity of their working together towards the common aim of increased prosperity for all seemed completely self-evident to Taylor. He was thus driven to asking: Why is there so much antagonism and inefficiency?

He suggests three causes: first, the fallacious belief of the workers that any increase in output would inevitably result in unemployment; second, the defective systems of management which make it necessary for workers to restrict output in order to protect their interests ('systematic soldiering'); third, inefficient rule-of-thumb effort-wasting methods of work. Taylor conceived it to be the aim of 'scientific management' to overcome these obstacles. This could be achieved by a systematic study of work to discover the most efficient methods of performing the job, and then a systematic study of management leading to the most efficient methods of controlling the workers. This would bring a great increase in efficiency and with it prosperity to the benefit of all, since a highly efficient prosperous business would be in a much better position to ensure the continuing well-paid employment of its workers. As Taylor put it: 'What the workmen want from their employers beyond anything else is high wages and what employers want from their workmen most of all is low labour cost of manufacture . . . the existence or absence of these two elements forms the best index to either good or bad management.'

To achieve this Taylor lays down four 'great underlying principles of management':

THE DEVELOPMENT OF A TRUE SCIENCE OF WORK

He points out that we do not really know what constitutes a fair day's work; a boss therefore has unlimited opportunities for complaining about workers' inadequacies, and workers never really know what is expected of them. This can be remedied by the establishment after scientific investigation of a 'large daily task' as the amount to be done by a suitable worker under optimum conditions. For this they would receive a high rate of pay – much higher than the average worker would receive in 'unscientific' factories. They would also suffer a loss of income if they failed to achieve this performance.

THE SCIENTIFIC SELECTION AND PROGRESSIVE DEVELOPMENT OF THE WORKER

To earn this high rate of pay workers would have to be scientifically selected to ensure that they possess the physical and intellectual qualities to enable them to achieve the output. Then they must be systematically trained to be 'first-class'. Taylor believes that every worker could be first-class at some job. It was the responsibility of management to develop workers, offering them opportunities for advancement which would finally enable them to do 'the highest, most interesting and most profitable class of work' for which they could become 'first-class'.

THE BRINGING TOGETHER OF THE SCIENCE OF WORK AND THE SCIENTIFICALLY SELECTED AND TRAINED WORKERS

It is this process that causes the 'mental revolution' in management and Taylor maintains that almost invariably the major resistance to scientific management comes from the side of management. The workers, he finds, are very willing to cooperate in learning to do a good job for a high rate of pay.

THE CONSTANT AND INTIMATE COOPERATION OF MANAGEMENT AND WORKERS

There is an almost equal division of work and responsibility between management and workers. The management take over all the work for which they are better fitted than the workers, i.e. the specification and verification of the methods, time, price and quality standards of the job, and the continuous supervision and control of the workers doing it. As Taylor saw it, there should be hardly a single act done by any worker which is not preceded by and followed by some act on the part of management. With this close personal cooperation the opportunities for conflict are almost eliminated, since the operation of this authority is not arbitrary. The managers are continually demonstrating that their decisions are subject to the same discipline as the workers, namely the scientific study of the work.

By 'science' Taylor means systematic observation and measurement, and an example of his method that he often quotes is the development of 'the science of shovelling'. He is insistent that, although shovelling is a very simple job, the study of the factors affecting efficient shovelling is quite complex. So much so that a worker who is phlegmatic enough to be able to do the job and stupid enough to choose it is extremely unlikely to be able to develop the most efficient method alone. But this is in fact what is hoped will happen. The *scientific* study of shovelling involves the determination of the optimum load that a 'first-class' worker can handle with each shovelful. Then the correct size of shovel to obtain this load, with different materials, must be established. Workers must be provided with a range of shovels and told which one to use. They must then be placed on an incentive payment scheme which allows them to earn high wages (double what they would earn in 'unscientific' firms) in return for high output.

The insistence on maximum specialization, and the removal of all extraneous elements in order to concentrate on the essential task, is fundamental to Taylor's thinking. He applies this concept to management too. He considers that the work of a typical factory supervisor is composed of a number of different functions (such as cost clerk, time clerk, inspector, repair boss, shop disciplinarian) and he believes that these could be separated out and performed by different specialists who would each be responsible for controlling different aspects of the work and the workers. He calls this system 'functional management' and likens the increased efficiency that it would bring to that obtained in a school where classes go to specialist teachers for different subjects, compared with a school in which one teacher teaches all subjects. He also formulates 'the exception principle' which lays down that management reports should be condensed into comparative summaries giving in detail only the exceptions to past standards or averages – both the especially good and the especially bad exceptions. Thus the manager would obtain an immediate and comprehensive view of the progress of the work.

Taylor's methods have been followed by many others, among them Gantt, Frank and Lillian Gilbreth, Bedaux, Rowan and Halsey. They have developed his thinking into what is now called Work Study or Industrial Engineering. But even in his lifetime Taylor's ideas led to bitter controversy over the alleged inhumanity of his system, which was said to reduce workers to the level of efficiently functioning machines. In fairness to Taylor, it must be said that his principles were often inadequately understood. For example, few managements have been willing to put into practice one of his basic tenets – that there should be no limit to the earnings of a high-producing worker; many incentive schemes involve such limits. This may inhibit the 'mental revolution' Taylor sought, which requires that 'both sides take their eyes off the division of the surplus as the all important matter and together turn their attention towards increasing the size of the surplus'.

BIBLIOGRAPHY

TAYLOR, F. W., *Scientific Management*, Harper & Row, 1947.

AITKEN, H. G. J., *Taylorism at Watertown Arsenal*, Harvard University Press, 1960.

Harry Braverman and the 'Labour Process' Debate

Harry Braverman (1920–1976) was an American Marxist theorist who was concerned to analyse the effects of the modern capitalist economy on the organization of work. He was stimulated to this by what he regarded as the unrealistic nature of much of what was written about productive labour. Braverman himself had very practical experience to bring to his analysis: he was trained as a craftsman coppersmith, and worked at that trade and at pipe fitting and sheet-metal work. He was employed in a naval shipyard, a railroad repair shop and two sheet steel plants – in all of which he experienced the impact of technological change on craft employment. In later years as a journalist, book editor then publishing executive, he again had experience of the impact of modern technology, this time on administrative work such as marketing, accounting and book production routines. His basic thesis is that in a capitalist economy all these changes act to de-skill work and to remove more and more power away from workers and into the hands of owners and managers. His book expounding this theme, *Labour and Monopoly Capitalism: the Degradation of Work in the Twentieth Century*, was awarded the 1974 C. Wright Mills Prize of the Society for the Study of Social Problems.

Braverman uses the framework for analysing the nature of the capitalist system presented by Karl Marx in *Capital*, Volume 1 (published in 1867), and applies it to modern work and its organization. Marx used the term the 'labour process' to refer to the ways by which raw materials are transformed into goods by human labour using tools and machines. In a capitalist system, by definition, the tools and machines are not owned by the workers but by the capitalists, and so the resulting goods become commodities to be sold on the market for the owners' profit. Workers themselves also have only a commodity to offer: their labour in exchange for wages. In this system it is inevitable that owners will 'exploit' workers (i.e. obtain as much as possible as a contribution to profit while paying as little as possible in return as wages).

In modern terms, according to Braverman, this requires managers (as representatives of owners) to design and redesign work in order to achieve competitive levels of profit. They need to have maximum control of workers and to be looking continually for ways of increasing that control. Typically, this has been achieved by increasing the division of labour into smaller and smaller, less and less demanding fragments of tasks. In this way increased output may be obtained from a workforce which is cheaper, since it is less skilled and less trained. Ford-type mass production epitomizes the results. Car workers on an assembly line, for example, who drive to their place of work, will have already exercised their highest level of skill for that day.

This de-skilling and the abolition of craft ownership of work leads to alienation. This is another reason for the owning class (and its representatives – the managers) to need to control the working class. They are seen as untrustworthy members of an opposing class who are likely to obstruct, undermine, or otherwise resist the legitimate capitalist objective of maximizing profit. From this point of view, ways of organizing the labour and production process are not rationally determined in order to increase objective efficiencey: rather organizations take the form they do in order to enhance the domination of capital over labour.

The prime advocate of this approach to efficiency in the organization of production was F. W. Taylor (see p. 90). Braverman sees 'Scientific Management', so-called, as the classic and inevitable method used to control labour in growing capitalist enterprises. It is, of course, not scientific since it does not attempt to discover what is the actual case, but accepts management's view that it has a refractory workforce which has to be kept under control. It is not a 'science of work' but a 'science of the management of others' work under capitalist conditions'. Its three basic tenets are: that knowledge of the labour process must be gathered in one place, that it must be the exclusive preserve of management and not available to the workers, and that this monopoly of knowlege must be used by management to control each step of the labour process. In total contrast to craft working, Taylor advocated a complete separation of conception from execution.

Braverman insists that Scientific Management is in full flow as the dominant approach to capitalist organization of the labour process. He is very dismissive of those social science writers of the 'human relations' approach (see Mayo p. 152, Likert and McGregor p. 156, Herzberg p. 176, etc.) who maintain the need to humanize work and improve the quality of working life. In industry these ideas are relegated to the sidelines of the personnel and training departments, with little real impact on the management of worker or work. In the production departments where the labour process is actually carried out and controlled, Taylorism reigns supreme. It is indeed being extended to an even wider range of occupations, such as clerical and administrative routines which are continually being de-skilled with the use of new computer technology. Braverman rejects the idea that automation is qualitatively different in the skill demands it makes of workers, as compared to mechanization. He argues that it, too, will decrease skill, as will any other technological development. This result is not a matter of a particular technology, but of how it is inevitably used to increase the control of the labour process by capital in the interests of profit.

The de-skilling, and cheapening, of such 'white collar' jobs as those of clerks and computer operators, leads to an increase in the alienated working class. In the situation of 'monopoly capitalism' (i.e. where giant corporations control the markets), new commodities are brought into being to shape the consumer to the needs of capital. All of society becomes a gigantic market place in the pursuit of profit. Printing and television, for example, become vehicles largely for marketing rather than for information and education. Thus, there is not only the degradation of work but also the degradation of family and community.

In the aftermath of Braverman's book, Marxist sociologists have been discussing its adequacy. Two particular issues have been taken up. The first concerns the inevitability of de-skilling on Taylorist lines in capitalist production. Braverman argued that it was the one classic form which gave cheapness and control in the labour process, and therefore was the inevitable result. Later writers have suggested that de-skilling may not be universal and work under capitalism can take a variety of forms. Managements may use different ways to achieve their objectives of control. Richard Edwards in an historical survey of workplace relations, argues that, although a hierarchy has remained constant, various additional forms of control have been used (e.g. coercive, technical, bureaucratic) depending upon the struggle of owners, workers and others to protect and advance their interests.

A second criticism has focused on Braverman's argument that the deskilling of white collar workers will lead to an increase in the working class. As Graeme Salaman argues, this neglects the important element of subjective identification of workers. This means that even de-skilled administrators and computer operators, for example, consider themselves – and therefore act and vote – as middle class.

BIBLIOGRAPHY

BRAVERMAN, H., *Labour and Monopoly Capitalism: the Degradation of Work in the Twentieth Century*, Monthly Review Press, 1974.

EDWARDS, R., *Contested Terrain: the Transformation of the Workplace in the Twentieth Century*, Heinemann, 1979.

SALAMAN, G., *Working*, Tavistock Publications, 1986.

Peter F. Drucker

Peter Drucker was born in Austria. He qualified in law and was a journalist in Germany until the advent of the Nazis. After a period in London, he moved to New York in 1937. He has been an economic consultant to banks and insurance companies and an adviser on business policy and management to a large number of American corporations. His many books on business topics have made him one of the leading contemporary writers on management policy issues. He was for many years at New York University Business School and since 1971 has been Clarke Professor of Social Science at Claremont Graduate School, California.

Drucker's work begins with a view of top management and its critical role in the representative institution of modern industrial society, namely the large corporation. Following from this he identifies management as the central problem area, and managers as the dynamic element in every business. It is managers through their control of the decision-making structure of the modern corporation who breathe life into the organization and the society. Managers are given human and material resources to work with, and from them fashion a productive enterprise from which springs the wealth of the society. This is becoming increasingly true as we move into an era of knowledge technology, making human resources ever more central to effective performance in organizations. Yet as Drucker points out, managers, while becoming ever more basic resources of a business, are increasingly the scarcest, the most expensive and the most perishable. Given this, it becomes extremely important that managers should be used as effectively as possible at the present state of knowledge about the practice and functions of management. It is to the problem of managerial effectiveness that Drucker addresses himself.

It is only possible to arrive at prescriptions for effectiveness if we first understand the role of the manager in the organization; if we know what the job of management is. There are, says Drucker, two dimensions to the task of management, an economic dimension and a time dimension. Managers are responsible for business organizations (this distinguishes them from administrators generally). As such they must always put economic performance first; the final standard for judging them is economic performance, which of course is not the case for all administrators. The second dimension, time, is one which is present in all decision-making systems. Management always has to think of the impact of a decision on the present, the short term future and the long term future. This is, of course, tied in with the economic aspect. Taken together it means that managers are evaluated in terms of their economic performance in the present, the short term and the long term.

Management, then, is the job of organizing resources to achieve satisfactory performance; to produce an enterprise from material and human resources. According to Drucker this does not necessarily mean profit maximization. For him profit is not the cause of business behaviour, or the rationale of business decision-making in the sense of always attempting to achieve the maximum profit. Rather profit is a test of the validity or success of the business enterprise. The aim of any business is to achieve sufficient profit, which will cover the risks that have been taken and avoid a loss.

The central question for Drucker is how best to manage a business to ensure that profits are made, and that the enterprise is successful over time. Although it is possible to state the overall aims in a fairly precise and simple way, any on-going functioning organization has a variety of needs and goals. It is not realistic to think of an enterprise having a single objective. Efficient management always involves a juggling act, balancing the different possible objectives, deciding the priorities to be put on the multiple aims that an organization has. Because of this, and due to the complex nature of business as exemplified by departmentalization, management by objectives is vital. This is essential in the process of ensuring that informed judgement takes place. It forces managers to examine available alternatives and provides a reliable means for evaluating management performance.

Specifically, objectives in a business enterprise enable management to explain, predict and control activities in a way which single ideas like profit maximization do not. First, they enable the organization to explain the whole range of business phenomena in a small number of general statements. Secondly, they allow the testing of these statements in actual experience. Thirdly, it becomes possible to predict behaviour. Fourthly, the soundness of decisions can be examined while they are still being made rather than after the fact. Fifthly, performance in the future can be improved as a result of the analysis of past experience. This is because objectives force one to plan in detail what the business must aim at and to work out ways of effectively achieving these aims. Management by Objectives (MbO) involves spelling out what is meant by managing a business. By doing this, and then examining the outcome over time the five advantages outlined above are realized.

But this still leaves the problem of what the objectives of a business enterprise should be. To quote Drucker: 'Objectives are needed in every area where performance and results directly and vitally affect the survival and prosperity of the business.' More concretely, there are eight areas in business where performance objectives must be set. These areas are: market standing; innovation; productivity; physical and financial resources; profitability; manager performance and development; worker performance and attitude; public responsibility. In deciding how to set objectives for these areas it is necessary to take account of possible measures and lay down a realistic time span. Measures are important because they make things visible and 'real'; they tell the manager what to focus attention upon. Unfortunately, measurement in most areas of business is still at a very crude level. As far as the time span of objectives is concerned, this depends on the area and the nature of the business. In the lumber business, today's plantings are the production capacity of fifty years' time; in parts of the clothing industry a few weeks' time may be the 'long-range future'.

But perhaps the most important part of MbO is the effect that it has on the individual manager. It enables the organization to develop its most important resource, management. This is because managerial self-control is developed, leading to stronger motivation and more efficient learning. It is the essence of this style of management that all managers arrive at a set of realistic objectives for their own units and for themselves. These objectives should spell out the contribution that the manager will make to the attainment of company goals in all areas of the business. It is always necessary that the objectives set should be checked by higher levels of management to make sure that they are attainable (neither too high nor too low). But the importance of individual managerial involvement in the setting of objectives, as a motivator, cannot be overstressed. If managers are really going to be able to improve their performance and take proper advantage of the system, they must be given direct information which will enable them to measure and evaluate their own achievements. This is very different from the situation in some companies where certain groups (e.g. accountants) act as the 'secret police' of the chief executive.

The necessity of individual managers setting their own objectives stems from the nature of modern business, and what Drucker calls three forces of misdirection. These are: the specialized work of most managers, the existence of a hierarchy, and the differences in vision that exist in businesses. All these raise the possibility of breakdown and conflicts in the organization. MbO is a way of overcoming these deficiencies by relating the task of each manager to the overall goals of the company. By doing this it takes note of an important aspect of modern business operations; management is no longer the domain of one person. Even the chief executive does not operate in isolation. Management is a group operation, and the existence of objectives emphasizes the contribution that each individual manager makes to the total group operation. The problem of a chief executive is that of picking the best managerial group; the existence of objectives with their built-in evaluation system enables better choices to be made.

Management by objectives, then, enables an executive to be effective. An important point is that effectiveness can be learned. Drucker insists that the self-development of effective executives is central to the continued development of the organization as the 'knowledge worker' becomes the major resource. The system of objectives allows managers to evaluate their own performance, and by doing so strengthens the learning process. It does this by showing where the particular strengths of the individual lie and how these can be made more productive (e.g. by reinforcing old priorities or establishing new ones, and by improving decision-making patterns). This regular review of objectives and performance enables managers to know where their most effective contributions are made and how they are made. As a result they are able to develop their skills in appropriate areas.

Overall then, MbO helps to overcome some of the forces which threaten to split the organization, by clearly relating the task of each manager to the overall aims of the company. It allows learning to take place and as a result the development of all managers to the best of their individual capacities. And finally, and most importantly, it increases the motivation of the managers and develops their commitment to the organization. The result is that organizational goals are reached by having common people achieve uncommon performance.

BIBLIOGRAPHY

DRUCKER, P. F., *The Practice of Management*, Harper & Row, 1954.
DRUCKER, P. F., *Managing for Results*, Harper & Row, 1964.
DRUCKER, P. F., *Managing in Turbulent Times*, Heinemann, 1980.
DRUCKER, P. F., *The Frontiers of Management*, Heinemann, 1987.

Thomas J. Peters and Robert H. Waterman

Tom Peters and Bob Waterman had been partners in McKinsey and Company, the leading management consultancy firm, for many years when they undertook a study of excellence in American business. Their report, *In Search of Excellence*, became the most popular management book of recent years with up to five million copies sold worldwide. Peters now runs his own organization founded to develop and propagate the ideas.

Peters and Waterman were concerned to examine and draw lessons from companies which were big (i.e. had annual turnovers of more than $1 bn.) and which were well established (i.e. more than twenty years old). From the *Fortune 500* list of the largest US companies, forty-three companies were chosen which satisfied a number of performance criteria. They had to be of above average growth and financial return over a twenty year period, plus having a reputation in their business sector for continuous innovation in response to changing markets. For all these firms, a full study of the published information on them over twenty-five years was carried out. In addition, about half the cases were the subject of extensive interview studies of the top managers involved; more limited interviews were conducted in the remaining half of the sample.

The companies designated to be excellent by this process include such leading names as Boeing, Hewlett-Packard, IBM, Johnson & Johnson, McDonald's, Proctor & Gamble and 3M. It is not claimed for these firms, and for the others classified as excellent, that they are without fault; they have made plenty of well publicized mistakes. But overall they have performed well over long periods, and they are in a good position to continue as innovative in the future.

The interviews were concerned with top management organizing for success and how it is tackled in these excellent companies. Peters and Waterman soon decided that they could not stick to the formal aspects of managing: the organization chart, the budget plan, the balance sheet, the control graph. These highly analytical tools and concepts are inherently conservative. They lead to detailed forecasting and planning, and tight control: cost reduction becomes the priority and not revenue enhancement, for example. Above all the philosophy behind the use of these narrowly rational techniques is to abhor mistakes, and therefore it does not value experimentation.

Such an approach cannot capture the distinctive nature of the excellent firms who innovate. A much wider range of processes must be considered. It must cover much that will be classified as informal, intuitive, irrational, intractable, but which cannot be ignored. Indeed it must be managed, as it has as much or more to do with the way companies excel (or fail), as do the formal structures and strategies.

Together with their colleagues Richard Pascale and Anthony Athos, Peters and Waterman developed a set of concepts to focus on what happens in the process of organizing which became known as the McKinsey 7-S Framework. This is a series of seven interdependent aspects of organizing – all conveniently beginning with the letter 's': structure, strategy, systems (and procedures), style (of management), skills (corporate strengths), staff (people) and shared values (culture). On the basis of this framework Peters and Waterman developed a set of eight attributes which characterize all excellent innovative US companies.

1. A BIAS FOR ACTION

Even though these companies may be analytical in their approach to decision making, they are not paralysed by the analysis. They have a 'can do' and 'let's try' approach which favours experimentation. Managers do not rely on the formal information and control systems. They get out of their offices and keep in touch informally; 'MBWA – Management By Wandering Around' it is called at Hewlett-Packard. An open door policy at all levels is typical, as is the organizational fluidity which allows the setting up of small task forces (mainly of volunteers) with short deadlines who are expected to come up with an answer to a problem *and then implement their proposals.*

2. CLOSE TO THE CUSTOMER

These companies offer good products because they do not regard the customer as a bloody nuisance, best ignored. They regularly listen to their customers from whom they get some of their best product ideas. They have what amounts to an obsession about customer service. IBM, for example, trains its salesmen not to be salesmen but 'customer problem solvers'. Its claim to give the best customer service of any company in the world is backed up by a fleet of special assistants (including some of the best salesmen) who are on three-year secondments doing only one thing – dealing with every customer complaint within twenty-four hours.

3. AUTONOMY AND ENTREPRENEURSHIP

The innovative companies foster many leaders and many innovators throughout the organization. 3M, for example, is a hive of 'product champions' who have been allowed to be creative and who are feverishly trying to make their idea successful. Top management does not try to control so tightly that everyone feels stifled. They support practical risk taking and they encourage internal competition. They have large numbers of innovations on the go and they can tolerate it when inevitably many fail – that is how they ensure that *some* succeed. The comparison with Burns's organic system of management (see p. 41) is very clear.

4. PRODUCTIVITY THROUGH PEOPLE

The excellent companies treat the ordinary members of the organization as the basic source of quality and productivity gains. They do not regard capital investment and labour substitution as the fundamental source of efficiency improvement. They strongly oppose an 'us–them' attitude in industrial relations and they treat workers as people. They are not soft; the people orientation has a tough side. They are very performance conscious, but the personal achievements stem from mutually high expectations and peer review rather than exhortation and complicated control systems.

McDonald's, for example, compare a well-run restaurant to a winning baseball team and always refer to workers as 'crew members'. They believe that senior managers should be out in the field paying attention to employees, to training, to the standard of service offered. They work hard to restrain and cut the corporate management, believing that the less there is, the better. Their commitment to productivity through people is illustrated by the 'McDonald's Hamburger University' out of which many crew members graduate, and the annual competition for the best 'All-American Hamburger Maker'.

5. HANDS-ON, VALUE DRIVEN

The basic philosophy of the excellent firms, the shared values of all the participants, may sound very 'soft' and abstract, but it has far more to do with their achievements than economic resources, technological developments, organizational structure or control systems. All of these factors have to change over the years but the philosophy must be established and maintained from the top to bottom of the firm. Those at the top work hard to maintain the values in a very public hands-on way. Their chief executives are famed throughout the company for getting involved in the actual processes (design, selling, etc.) thus publically demonstrating their commitment to high standards.

This explicit understanding of, and commitment to, a system of values is probably the single most important key to excellence. Less successful firms either do not know what their values are, or have a set of objectives, but seem only to get fired up about quantitative ones (e.g. earnings per share, growth measures). These can motivate the top ten, fifty, even the top hundred managers, but larger firms need to propagate clear values throughout the whole organization. The content of the dominant beliefs is narrow in scope, but exhibited by all the firms. It includes a belief in being the best producer (whether the product is an aircraft, a hamburger or an advertising campaign) and in giving superior quality and service. The importance of the nuts and bolts of doing the job well, of informal methods of improving communication to achieve goals, of economic growth and profits, also feature strongly.

6. STICK TO THE KNITTING

Excellent companies do not wish to become conglomerates. 'Never acquire a business you don't know to run' was how a retiring chairman of Johnson & Johnson put it to his successor. They have seen the way corporations like ITT have suffered through trying to spread into new business sectors by large acquisition. Excellent companies move out mainly through internally generated diversification, one manageable step at a time.

7. SIMPLE FORM, LEAN STAFF

As big as these companies are, the underlying structural forms and systems are elegantly simple. Top level staffs are lean: corporate staffs of fewer than a hundred people running multi-billion-dollar enterprises. Complicated structures which blur the lines of authority, such as matrix organization, are eschewed. The straightforward divisional form with the product divisions having all the functions of a business is used. The hiving off of successful new products into separate divisions is encouraged and rewarded at surprisingly small volumes (e.g. at about $20 m. turnover at 3M).

8. SIMULTANEOUS LOOSE–TIGHT PROPERTIES

The excellent companies are both centralized and decentralized. For the most part they have pushed autonomy downwards, to the division, to the product development team, to the shop floor. On the other hand they are fanatical centralists around the few core values they see as key to the enterprise: quality, reliability, action, regular informal communication, quick feedback. These are ways of exerting extremely tight control and ensuring that nothing gets very far out of line. The attention to the customer is one of the tightest properties of all – not through massive forms and large numbers of control variables but through self and peer discipline making this the focus of activity. Thus the 'soft' concept of a philosophical value is, in fact, harder in its impact than setting target ratios in a control system. As one chief executive said: 'It's easy to fool the boss, but you can't fool your peers.'

These findings, Peters and Waterman underline, show that the excellent companies were, above all, 'brilliant on the basics'. They do not let techniques substitute for thinking nor analysis impede action. They work hard to keep things simple in a complex world. They tolerate some chaos in return for quick action and regular innovation. They prize their values as their most essential asset.

One conclusion that Peters and Waterman came to, rather reluctantly, was that associated with almost every excellent company was a strong leader who was instrumental in forming the culture of excellence in the early stages of the firm's development. Even so, they strongly believe that firms can change towards excellence, and in later books Peters gives more examples of the working out of the approach, and proposes ways in which managers can move their organizations in that direction.

BIBLIOGRAPHY

PETERS, T. J., and WATERMAN, R. H., *In Search of Excellence: Lessons from America's Best-Run Companies*, Harper & Row, 1982.

PETERS, T. J., and AUSTIN, N., *A Passion for Excellence: The Leadership Difference*, Collins, 1985.

PETERS, T. J., *Thriving on Chaos: A Handbook for Management Revolution*, Macmillan, 1988.

William Ouchi

William Ouchi is an American professor of Japanese extraction who works at the Graduate School of Management, University of California, Los Angeles. For Ouchi the key issue facing American (and generally Western) business is how its managers will react to one fact – 'the Japanese know how to manage better than we do'.

Ouchi and his collaborators have carried out detailed studies of the way in which Japanese companies operate, both in Japan and in the United States. He has identified a particular Japanese organizational culture (related to, and deriving from, the general culture of Japanese society) which is more conducive to greater productivity than typical western organizational cultures.

He characterizes that work culture by using words which may sound abstract, 'soft', even 'wet' to western managerial ears but whose working out is the key to Japanese success. In comparison to western firms, Japanese organizational culture is based on more trust, more subtlety and more intimacy in work relationships.

Japanese workers and managers trust their superiors considerably more than western employees do and this is an important key to productivity and growth. For example, both American and Japanese managers want to be successful, but for the Japanese this means taking a much longer-term view. For an American, success might be a healthy bottom-line figure at the end of this financial quarter, even if it causes problems or losses in other parts of the organization: 'that's their problem!' might be a typical reaction. Japanese managers are willing to accept sacrifices if the firm's overall profitability will be maximized, trusting in the knowledge that they will achieve recognition and recompense in future opportunities. In any case, their take home salary will be affected by the overall performance of the firm, not their particular section of it.

Greater subtlety in relationships is demonstrated by superiors who know the personalities of their staff and can use this knowledge to put together work teams of maximal effectiveness, without being hampered by professional or trade-union work rigidities. Intimacy is shown by the caring, the support, and the disciplined unselfishness which make possible effective social life even at work. In the west, this characteristic has traditionally been thought appropriate to the family only, perhaps with the addition of a few lifelong friends. In Japan with the tradition of lifelong employment, economic and social life are integrated into a whole. People who live in a company dormitory, play in a company sports team, serve on the same company committees and working parties and know that they will continue to do so for the rest of their working lives, necessarily become more intimate in taking account of each other. They cannot, for example, afford selfish and dishonest behaviour, since they have to live long and closely with the consequences.

The most important characteristic of Japanese organization is lifetime employment, since it is the rubric under which many facets of life and work are integrated. Lifetime employment, although desired by workers and a goal of employers, is not universal in Japan. It applies to male employees only; women are expected to retire on marriage. Even for males, not all firms can create the economic stability necessary to support such a system, but all large companies and government departments operate it. A pool of new employees is recruited by an organization straight from school and University once a year, even though there is typically not work for all of them immediately. Thereafter, promotion is entirely from within, and those with experience of one company will not be considered for employment by another. Once hired, the new employee will remain with the company until the mandatory retirement age of fifty-five. This relatively low age acts to create opportunities for younger people to progress. Until retirement, an employee will not be dismissed for anything less than a major criminal offence, and dismissal is a harsh punishment since such a person has no possibility of finding work in a comparable major organization, and must turn to small low-wage firms.

So, the pressures to be aware of what the organization requires and fit in with it are very strong. And for a manager they do not stop at age fifty-five. On retirement, managers, in addition to getting a lump sum gratuity, are placed in one of the satellite supply firms which surround each major company. The job there, a part-time one for about ten years, would be to help ensure that the supplies are to the quality and time required by the major firm. It is an important task since the firm relies on one supplier completely for each particular component; there is no concept of dual sourcing of supplies.

This approach is very different from that in the west, with its labour markets for all levels of jobs and experience, and changes between firms being perfectly acceptable. The existence of these labour markets requires that managers particularly look for opportunities for rapid promotion, and with this must go relatively rapid evaluation of performance.

On the other hand, Japanese managers (male, with extremely rare exceptions) have the security of lifelong employment. They are part of a system which has a very slow performance and evaluation pattern. For the first ten years of his organizational life, a manager there will expect to receive the same increases in pay and the same promotions as the others who entered the firm at the same time as he did. This discourages short-term 'games' since the manager has no reason to promote his career at someone else's expense, and encourages an open attitude to cooperation. The typical open-plan nature of the Japanese office with several managerial levels in the same room, also encourages openness since everybody can see who is interacting with whom, who is listened to, who has influence, and so on.

Lifelong employment also allows non-specialized career paths. A beginning manager will be sent to serve in all the departments of the business. Not just on a short period of secondment before sticking to a specialism as in some western traineeships, but a varied career progression lasting several decades. In the west this might well hamper a manager, who will not have sufficient experience in a specialism on which to enter the job market. Generalists, with a great knowledge of one company and its workings in many areas, are not so marketable to other companies. In Japan they do not need to be.

One important effect of the generalist experience, combined with a method of payment which is based on company-wide – not personal or departmental – achievement, is that organization structures can be much more flexible. There is much less emphasis on who precisely is responsible for a particular operation and much greater emphasis on communication and decision making by consensus. There is an intentional ambiguity about decision making which encourages collective responsibility. Important decisions, therefore, take longer to make since all the managers who would be affected are consulted about possible options. Consensus when it is achieved in this fashion generates a great deal of commitment. This is physically manifested in the fact that, for example, a document proposing a change in procedures may typically show the seal of approval of twenty or more managers before the Director puts his final seal on it.

These manifestations of collective values run throughout Japanese organizational culture. It is an obvious fact of life to the Japanese that everything important happens as a result of teamwork and collective effort. By American standards, Japanese cost and managerial accounting systems are relatively underdeveloped. Profit centres, transfer pricing, the untangling and allocation of costs of common services to particular departments, are much less important in Japanese firms. The overall achievement is paramount, not the relative position of the component parts.

A US company operating in Japan found that its suggestion scheme did not work until it withdrew its American practice of rewarding the individual who made the suggestion and offered instead a group bonus.

This is used by the group together for a family party or group vacation, underlining the holistic concern of the culture.

The Japanese model of organization is thus very different from the American model in every important respect, as is summarized by the following list:

Japanese organizations	*American organizations*
Lifetime employment	Short-term employment
Slow evaluation and promotion	Rapid evaluation and promotion
Non-specialized career paths	Specialized career paths
Implicit control mechanisms	Explicit control mechanisms
Collective decision making	Individual decision making
Collective responsibility	Individual responsibility
Holistic concern	Segmented concern

American and western organizations cannot turn into Japanese ones – and would not want to, because in their much more individually-orientated culture they would find much of the collective emphasis stifling. Are there, however, elements of the Japanese style that can be sensibly applied in the west? Ouchi thinks there are. He recounts an occasion when he was describing the style and got the response from one manager: 'Do you realise that IBM is exactly like that?' Other companies which have been suggested as having *some* of these characteristics include Proctor & Gamble, Eastman–Kodak, the armed forces and many smaller firms.

Ouchi uses the term 'Theory Z' to describe the Japanese model as adapted to the west. His terminology relates to the 'Theory X' and 'Theory Y' of Douglas McGregor (see p. 156). Theory Z builds on and goes beyond McGregor's Theory Y, by using insights from the workings of Japanese organizations. Thus, American Z organizations have long-term employment (though not necessarily lifelong, Japanese style), a large investment in the training of employees who thus develop specific company skills, and relatively slow promotion (by American standards – though nothing like the ten years of the Japanese). Although they have financial and operational analyses, they use 'soft' information a great deal in making decisions and pay much attention to whether an option is 'suitable' in that it fits in with the culture of the company. This 'fitting-in' is very important and they are much more homogeneous in their management groups, and take a more holistic and egalitarian view of them.

On the other hand, Z organizations find it very difficult to change except by modifying their cultures which takes time. They inevitably experience a loss of professionalism, and they tend to be more sexist and racist in recruitment, since they look to employ people like themselves. Even so, they are among the long-term organizational successes and are among the 'feeder' companies that head-hunters look to, knowing that they develop an uncommonly high proportion of their young people into successful general managers.

BIBLIOGRAPHY

OUCHI, W., *Theory Z: How American Business Can Meet the Japanese Challenge*, Addison-Wesley, 1981.

Rosabeth Moss Kanter

Rosabeth Moss Kanter is a Professor of Business Administration at the Harvard Business School and a consultant to many organizations. A sociologist working in the tradition of Max Weber (see p. 5), she has carried out a historical study of American work communes. She has been the recipient of a Guggenheim Fellowship, and a McKinsey Award for a 1979 article in the *Harvard Business Review* on 'Power Failure in Management Circuits'. Her detailed study of the human aspects of the functioning of a major present-day US manufacturing company, *Men and Women of the Corporation*, was the 1977 winner of the C. Wright Mills award for the best book on social issues.

The study focused on three key roles in the company (codenamed the Industrial Supply Corporation – 'Indsco'): those of managers, secretaries and wives. The managers, with a small minority of exceptions, were men; the secretaries and the wives were women, and Kanter's work analyses their relationships. It might seem strange to consider wives as part of the corporation, but in fact (although not in theory) this is how they were defined and treated. On the other hand, the husbands of the, relatively rare, female managers were not put in this position, being considered to be independent of Indsco.

Managers, particularly as they rise to the top, are required to cope with increasing uncertainty. Greater routinization applies primarily to the lower levels; managers have to be allowed to exercise discretion. They are therefore the recipients of the owners' and main Board's trust. At Indsco, the top managers inevitably chose people like themselves in whom to put this trust. The managers spent a lot of time interacting with each other – between a third and a half of their time actually in meetings. Interacting with people like yourself is always easier, and there was a decided wish to avoid those with whom communication was felt to be uncomfortable. Deviants and non-conformists were suspect; those who dressed differently raised questions because of the messages they might be conveying. Predictability had the highest value. It was acceptable to be somewhat controversial, as long as the manager was consistent and fitted in with the basic values of hard work (staying late at the office if necessary or taking work home) and loyalty (being committed to a long-term career with the company).

The response to the uncertainties of performance and the need for easy communication are great pressures for management to become a closed circle. Homogeneity is the prime criterion for selection and social conformity a standard for conduct. Women were clearly put in the category of the incomprehensible and unpredictable and, with rare exceptions, were excluded. Many managers reported that they felt uncomfortable in dealing with them. 'It took more time', 'They changed their minds all the time', 'I'm always making assumptions that turn out to be wrong', were typical comments. Some managers were prepared to admit that this was really saying something about themselves, but this then became another example of their preference for dealing with their own kind.

The secretary had a very distinctive role in the Corporation. She has been defined as the 'office wife'. This is a revealing analogy because the term 'wife' denotes a traditional, not a bureaucratic relationship (using Weber's terms, see p. 5). The secretarial promotion ladder (a bureaucratic component of the role) was very short; most women got there before the age of thirty and were then stuck. The only way forward was a promotion in the status of her boss. This determined both the formal rank and the actual power of the secretary: the tasks remained more or less the same at all levels.

The secretary, therefore, had to live her organizational life through her boss. In Weber's terms this is the patrimonial traditional pattern, even though it is embedded in a formal bureaucratic system. Very untypically in a bureaucracy where people normally work with those just above and just below themselves in status and salary, the boss–secretary relationship allows two people working closely together to have very wide discrepancies in remuneration. The relationship encourages considerable dependency, and secretaries are expected to show loyalty and devotion to their bosses. They are expected to value non-material rewards such as prestige, personal feelings of being wanted and 'loved', and having a salary rather than wages (even though that salary may be less than many wages).

Although the corporate wife had no official employment relationship with Indsco, she still had a clear career progression. There were three phases, each with its own problems. The first was the technical phase, corresponding to the husband's specialist or early managerial job. At that stage he is engaged in a job, extremely demanding of time and energy, in which she can play no part. Conversely, he is under-involved at home, and she tends to leave him out of the activities there. This mutual exclusion is the major strain and resentment.

The second, managerial phase of the wife's career came when the husband entered middle and upper management and she was expected to perform social and hostess duties. At this stage her behaviour, her social adequacy, has a considerable bearing on the progress of her husband's career. Friendships are no longer just a personal matter but have business implications – as, for example, when an old friendship between two of the managers and their wives had to be dropped because one manager now far outranked the other. Gossip is important, and every wife is faced with the problem as to how far she is going to let her true feelings determine her social life, and how far to let her relationships be determined by company 'political' considerations.

The third career phase was the institutional one, with the husband at the top of the organization or in a position where he must represent it to the outside. Here the issue for both husband and wife is the public nature of almost all their activities. What for others would be defined as pleasure (playing golf, attending a symphony concert, giving a party) are part of the business, and indeed allowable for tax as a business expense. Charitable and community service activities, where the wife's role is especially prominent, may generate useful business. The corporation and its needs and relationships pervades the couple's whole life. Yet, because so much of the top manager's work is concerned with evaluating and being evaluated on personal grounds of trust and integrity, the wife is faced with the task of carrying out these activities as though they were highly personal, not ritualistic and contrived. Her job is to contribute to the image of her husband as a whole real man. Top wives have also to suppress their private beliefs, and one wife, for example, told how proud she was that she never at any time during her husband's career unburdened herself of her private views to anyone.

From her study of Indsco, Kanter sees three important general needs for change in the modern industrial corporation: improving the quality of working life (to stem the steady decrease in the numbers of those who say that their jobs are satisfying), creating equal employment opportunities for women and minorities, and opening opportunities for releasing aspirations for employees to make better use of their talents in contributing to the corporation. To achieve these objectives, changes in organization structures are needed.

One way to enhance opportunities would be to open the circle of management to promotion from a wider range of personnel (e.g. women, clerical workers). This should be based on their appraised competences to do such jobs, and ignore the segregated and restricted career paths which trap them into lower-level jobs. Changes would be required in the appraisal, promotion and career systems and in the design of jobs. Ways need to be found to create intermediate jobs which would act as career bridges into management.

Then empowering strategies, concerned with flattening the hierarchy, decentralization and creating autonomous work groups, are necessary. Number-balancing strategies would aim to raise the proportion of women and other minorities in higher jobs. It is important to combat tokenism by ensuring that several such group members, not just a single representative, are hired and later promoted at the same time. All these strategies for change are required if 'affirmative action' policies are to be effective.

But Kanter is well aware of the difficulties in getting change in large corporations and this led her on to a study of 'change masters' – corporate entrepreneurs who are capable of anticipating the need for, and of leading, productive change. She carried out an in-depth study of ten major companies, each with a well known reputation for progessive human resource policies. The companies included General Electric, General Motors, Honeywell, Polaroid and Wang Laboratories.

By examining in detail 115 innovations and the factors which encouraged them, Kanter found a crucial distinction between organizations which can and do innovate, and those whose style of thought is against change and prevents innovation. Innovative firms have an 'integrative' approach to problems. They have a willingness to see problems as wholes and in their solutions to move beyond received wisdom, to challenge establish practices. Entrepreneurial organizations are willing to operate at the edges of their competence, dealing with what they do not yet know (e.g. new investments, new markets, new products). They do not measure themselves by the standards of the past, but by their visions of the future.

They contrast very strongly with firms with a 'segmentalist' approach. These see problems as narrowly as possible, independently of their context. Companies like this are likely to have segmented structures: a large number of compartments strongly walled off from one another – production department from marketing department, corporate managers from divisional managers, management from labour, men from women. As soon as a problem is identified, it is broken up and the parts dealt with by the appropriate departments. Little or no effort is given to the problem as an integrated whole. As a segmentalist manager, you are not going to start dealing with others' aspects of the problem and you would regard it as a personal failure if they were to start worrying about yours. So entrepreneurial spirit is stifled and the solution is unlikely to be innovative. It will follow the solid structure laid down. (This analysis is comparable to the organic versus mechanistic distinction of Burns, see p. 41.)

In describing cases of integrative organizations where innovations thrive, Kanter suggests a number of important elements necessary to reduce the segmentalism apparent in so many non-innovative, older, troubled firms. The aim is to reawaken the spirit of enterprise and arouse the potential entrepreneurs that exist in all organizations. The methods include encouragement of a culture of pride in the firm's own achievements, reduction of layers in the hierarchy, improvement of *lateral* communication, and giving of increased information about company plans. Decentralization is very important; as is the empowerment of entrepreneurial people lower down the organization to have the authority and the resources to exploit their ideas – even if this means cutting across established segments and boundaries.

BIBLIOGRAPHY

KANTER, R. M., *Men and Women of the Corporation*, Basic Books, 1977.

KANTER, R. M., 'Power Failure in Management Circuits', *Harvard Business Review* (July–August 1979), 65–75; reprinted in D. S. Pugh (ed.), *Organization Theory*, Penguin, 1990.

KANTER, R. M., *The Change Masters: Corporate Entrepreneurs at Work*, Allen and Unwin, 1984.

4 Decision-making in Organizations

The task of administration is so to design this environment that the individual will approach as close as practicable to rationality (judged in terms of the organization's goals) in his decisions.
HERBERT A. SIMON

An organization is a collection of choices looking for problems, issues and feelings looking for decision situations in which they might be aired, solutions looking for issues to which they might be the answers, and decision-makers looking for work.
JAMES G. MARCH

An administrator often feels more confident when 'flying by the seat of his pants' than when following the advice of theorists.
CHARLES E. LINDBLOM

It makes more sense to talk about participative and autocratic situations than it does to talk about participative and autocratic managers.
VICTOR H. VROOM

An organization can be considered as a set of games between groups of partners who have to play with each other.
MICHEL CROZIER

Hierarchy is divisive, it creates resentment, hostility and opposition . . . Paradoxically, through participation management increases its control by giving up some of its authority.
ARNOLD S. TANNENBAUM

Although writers have considered a range of aspects of organizational functioning, there has been a continuing school of thought which maintains that it is the analysis of decision-making which is the key to understanding organizational management processes.

This approach was inaugurated by Herbert Simon and his colleagues of Carnegie-Mellon University. For Simon, management is decision-making. His colleague James March develops this approach to consider the non-rationality of decision processes, while Charles Lindblom looks at decision-making in relation to public policy and discovers a 'science of muddling through'.

Victor Vroom proposes a theory of appropriate decision-making styles, Michel Crozier examines the nature of the power which is at the basis of the decision-making 'game', and Arnold Tannenbaum analyses the distribution across organizational levels of the power to control decision-making.

Herbert A. Simon

Herbert Simon is a distinguished American political and social scientist whose perceptive contributions have influenced thinking and practice in many fields. He began his career in public administration and operations research, but as he took appointments in successive universities his interests encompassed all aspects of administration. He is Professor of Computer Science and Psychology at Carnegie-Mellon University, Pittsburgh, where he and his colleagues have been engaged on fundamental research into the processes of decision-making, using computers to simulate human thinking. Herbert Simon's outstanding intellectual contribution was publicly recognized when, in 1978, he was awarded the Nobel Prize for Economics.

For Simon 'management' is equivalent to 'decision-making' and his major interest has been an analysis of how decisions are made and of how they might be made more effectively.

He describes three stages in the overall process of making a decision:

1. Finding occasions calling for a decision – the *intelligence* activity (using the word in the military sense).
2. Inventing, developing and analysing possible courses of action – the *design* activity.
3. Selecting a particular course of action from those available – the *choice* activity.

Generally speaking, intelligence activity precedes design, and design activity precedes choice; but the sequence of stages can be much more complex than this. Each stage in itself can be a complex decision-making process. The design stage can call for new intelligence activities. Problems at any stage can generate a series of sub-problems which in turn have their intelligence, design and choice stages. Nevertheless, in the process of organizational decision-making these three general stages can be discerned.

Carrying out the decisions is also regarded as a decision-making process. Thus after a policy decision has been taken, the executive having to carry it out is faced with a wholly new set of problems involving decision-making. Executing policy amounts to making more detailed policy. Essentially, for Simon, all managerial action is decision-making.

On what basis do administrators make decisions? The traditional theory of economists assumed complete rationality. Their model was of 'economic man' (which, of course, embraced woman) who deals with the real world in all its complexity. He selects the rationally determined best course of action from among all those available to him in order to maximize his returns. But clearly this model is divorced from reality. We know that there is a large non-rational element in people's thinking and behaviour. The need for an administrative theory is precisely because there are practical limits to human rationality. These limits to rationality are not static but depend upon the organizational environment in which the individual's decision takes place. It then becomes the task of administration so to design this environment that the individual will approach as close as practicable to rationality in decisions, as judged in terms of the organization's goals.

In place of 'economic man' Simon proposes a model of 'administrative man'. While economic man maximizes (i.e. selects the best course from those available), administrative man 'satisfices' – looking for a course of action that is satisfactory or 'good enough'. In this process decision-makers are content with gross simplifications, taking into account only those comparatively few relevant factors which their minds can manage to encompass. 'Most human decision-making, whether individual or organizational, is concerned with the discovery and selection of satisfactory alternatives; only in exceptional cases is it concerned with the discovery and selection of optimal alternatives.' Most decisions are concerned not with searching for the sharpest needle in the haystack but with searching for a needle sharp enough to sew with. Thus administrators who 'satisfice' can make decisions without searching for all the possible alternatives and can use relatively simple rules of thumb. In business terms they do not look for 'maximum profit' but 'adequate profit'; not 'optimum price' but 'fair price'. This makes their world much simpler.

What techniques of decision-making are then available? In discussing this problem, Simon makes a distinction between two polar types of decisions: *programmed* and *non-programmed* decisions. These are not mutually exclusive but rather make up a continuum stretching from highly programmed decisions at one end to highly unprogrammed decisions at the other. Decisions are programmed to the extent that they are repetitive and routine or a definite procedure has been worked out to deal with them. They thus do not have to be considered afresh each time they occur. Examples would be the decisions involved in processing a customer's order, determining an employee's sickness benefit or carrying out any routine job.

Decisions are unprogrammed to the extent that they are new and unstructured or where there is no cut-and-dried method for handling the problem. This may be either because it has not occurred before, or because it is particularly difficult or important. Examples would be decisions to introduce a new product, make substantial staff redundancies or move to a new location. All these decisions would be non-programmed (although entailing many programmed sub-decisions) because the organization would have no detailed strategy to govern its responses to these situations, and it would have to fall back on whatever general capacity it had for intelligent problem-solving.

Human beings are capable of acting intelligently in many new or difficult situations but they are likely to be less efficient. The cost to the organization of relying on non-programmed decisions in areas where special-purpose procedures and programmes can be developed is likely to be high and an organization should try to programme as many of its decisions as possible. The traditional techniques of programmed decision-making are habit, including knowledge and skills, clerical routines and standard operating procedures, and the organization's structure and culture, i.e. its system of common expectations, well-defined information channels, established sub-goals, etc. The traditional techniques for dealing with non-programmed decisions rely on the selection and training of executives who possess judgement, intuition and creativity. These categories of technique have been developed over thousands of years (the building of the pyramids must have involved the use of many of them). But since the Second World War, Simon argues, a complete revolution in techniques of decision-making has got under way, comparable to the invention of powered machinery in manufacture.

This revolution has been due to the application of such techniques as mathematical analysis, operational research, electronic data processing, information technology and computer simulation. These were used first for completely programmed operations (e.g. mathematical calculations, accounting procedures) formerly regarded as the province of clerks. But more and more elements of judgement (previously unprogrammed and the province of middle management) can now be incorporated into programmed procedures. Decisions on stock control and production control have been in the forefront of this development. With advances in computer technology, more and more complex decisions will become programmed. Even a completely unprogrammed decision, made once and for all, can be reached via computer techniques by building a model of the decision situation. Various courses of action can then be simulated and their effects assessed. 'The automated factory of the future', Simon maintains, 'will operate on the basis of programmed decisions produced in the automated office beside it.'

BIBLIOGRAPHY

SIMON, H. A., *Administrative Behaviour*, 2nd edn, Macmillan, 1960.

SIMON, H. A., *The New Science of Management Decision*, Harper & Row, 1960.

SIMON, H. A., *The Shape of Automation*, Harper & Row, 1965.

MARCH, J. G., and SIMON, H. A., *Organizations*, Wiley, 1958.

James G. March

James March is Professor of Management at Stanford University, California. His breadth of mind is indicated by his being linked also with the departments of Political Science and of Sociology. His interests have long focused upon decision-making in organizations, ever since his early work at Carnegie-Mellon University. Its renowned contributors to the understanding of decision-making include also Herbert Simon (see p. 119) and Richard Cyert, both colleagues of March and both still at Carnegie-Mellon, Cyert for many years as its President.

March himself brings to his lively analyses of decision-making a unique blend of the logical and the poetical. His work is logical in argument, poetical in imagery and expression. He feels that decision-making can be understood in much the same non-rational way as a painting by Picasso or a poem by T. S. Eliot. It is far from a rationally controlled process moving steadily to a culminating choice. The confusion and complexity surrounding decision-making is underestimated. Many things are happening at once. Views and aims are changing, and so are alliances between those concerned. What has to be done is not clear, nor is how to do it. In this topsy-turvy world where people do not comprehend what is going on, decisions may have little to do with the processes that supposedly make them, and organizations 'do not know what they are doing'.

It is a world in which there are cognitive, political, and organizational limits to rationality. Cognitively, attention is the key scarce resource. Individuals cannot attend to everything at once, nor can they be everywhere at once. So they attend to some parts of some decision-making, not to all of it. What they attend to depends upon the alternative claims upon them, since giving attention to one decision means overlooking others. As March puts it, 'every entrance is an exit somewhere else'. Therefore timing is crucial, timing when to join in and which matters to raise.

March shares with his former colleague Simon the conception of *bounded* rationality. Not only is attention scarce, mental capacity is limited. The mind of the decision-maker can only encompass so much. It can only cope with a limited amount of information, and with a limited number of alternatives (see also Lindblom, p. 128). That being so, even if decision-making is intended to be rational, there are severe bounds to its rationality. Decisions will be taken knowing much less than in principle could be known.

Along with scarce attention and bounded rationality come erratic preferences. People change their minds as to what they want. Even if they know what they want, they may ignore their own preferences and follow other advice or other traditions. They may state their preferences in an ambiguous way. Their preference may conflict with the preferences of others.

Here the cognitive limits to rationality connect with the political limits. March and his other former colleague Cyert recognize that a firm, and indeed any other kind of organization, is a shifting multiple-goal political coalition. 'The composition of the firm is not given; it is negotiated. The goals of the firm are not given; they are bargained.' The coalition, to use their word, includes managers, workers, stockholders, suppliers, customers, lawyers, tax collectors and other agents of the state, as well as all the sub-units or departments into which an organization is divided. Each have their own preferences about what the firm should be like and what its goals should be. Hence negotiation and bargaining rather than detached rationality are endemic.

This is where the political limits to rationality connect with the organizational limits. These are the limits set by *organized anarchies*. Though all organizations do not have the properties of organized anarchy all of the time, they do for part of the time, and especially if they are publicly owned or are educational such as universities, colleges and schools. Organized anarchies have 'three general properties'. First, since preferences are unclear, the organization discovers its goals from what it is doing rather than by defining them clearly in advance. Second, since it has 'unclear technology', 'its own processes are not understood by its members' and it works by trial and error more than by knowing what it is doing. Third, since there is 'fluid participation', who is involved in what is constantly changing. Take a college, for instance. Pronouncements on strategy are more reviews of what courses are already taught than they are statements of future goals; new teaching techniques such as video games are tried without knowing whether they will work and without their being understood by authorizing committees; and what such committees understand and approve depends on who turns up to meetings.

Given these cognitive, political and organizational characteristics, decision-making processes are bound to be affected. Not only in those organizations prone to organized anarchy, but even in business firms such decision processes have four peculiarities. They are:

1. Quasi-resolution of conflict
2. Uncertainty avoidance
3. Problemistic search
4. Organizational learning

Quasi-resolution of conflict is the state of affairs most of the time. The conflicts inherent in the political nature of organizations and therefore in the making of decisions are not resolved. Rather there are devices for their quasi-resolution which enable them to be lived with. One such device is 'local rationality'. Since each sub-unit or department deals only with a narrow range of problems – the sales department with 'how to sell' and the personnel department with 'how to recruit' and so on – each can at least purport to be rational in dealing with its 'local' concerns. Of course, these local rationalities can be mutually inconsistent (as when accounting's insistence on remaining within budget destroys marketing's advertising campaign), so they may not add up to overall rationality for the organization as a whole.

A second such device can ease this difficulty. It is 'acceptable level decision rules'. The acceptable level of consistency between one decision and another is low enough for the divergences to be tolerable. What is needed is an outcome acceptable to the different interests rather than one that is optimal overall. Third, 'sequential attention to goals' also helps. As the conflicts between goals are not resolved, attention is given first to one goal and then to another in sequence. For example, smooth production is first emphasized, then later on the priority switches to satisfying customers by design variations which disrupt production.

Uncertainty avoidance, too, pervades decision-making. All organizations must live with uncertainty. Customer orders are uncertain, so are currency fluctuations, so is future taxation, and so on. Therefore, decision-making responds to information here and now, and avoids the uncertainties of longer-term forecasting. Pressing problems are dealt with, and planning for the longer run is avoided. Market uncertainties are avoided by exclusive contracts with customers, and by conforming with everyone else to recognized pricing and negotiating practices. For the same reason *search is problemistic* and short-sighted. The occurrence of a problem spurs a search for ways to deal with it, and once a way is found then search stops. Far-sighted regular search, such as the steady accumulation of market information, is relatively unimportant. Such information is likely to be ignored in the urgency of any particular sales crisis. Moreover, search is 'simple-minded'. When a problem arises, search for a solution is concentrated near the old solution. Radical proposals are brushed aside and a safer answer is found not much different from what there was before (see Lindblom, p. 128). When an

American university sought a new dean to head a major faculty, prominent outsiders were passed over and an established insider chosen because of fears that outsiders might make too many changes. Business organizations, too, regularly choose both managers and workers to fit in with the least disruption to existing set-ups.

Finally, decision-making processes are learning processes. In them, *organizational learning* takes place. Decision-makers do not begin by knowing all they need to know. They learn as they go. They learn what is thought practicable and what is not, what is permissible and what is not. By trial and error they find out what can be done and adapt their goals to it.

Perhaps it should not be surprising that all this leads March, together with Cohen and Olsen, to propose a *garbage can model of organizational choice*, famed for its name as well as for what it postulates. For when people fight for the right to participate in decision-making and then do not exercise it, when they request information and then do not use it, when they struggle over a decision and then take little interest in whether it is ever carried out, something curious must be going on.

So, the opportunity or the need to arrive at a decision, to make a choice, can be seen as 'a garbage can into which various kinds of problems and solutions are dumped by participants as they are generated'. There may be several garbage cans around with different labels on.

In the model so vividly depicted, a decision is an outcome of the interplay between *problems*, *solutions*, *participants* and *choices*, all of which arrive relatively independently one of another. Problems can arise inside or outside the organization. Solutions exist on their own irrespective of problems (people's preferences wait for their moment to come, the computer waits for the question it can answer). Participants move in and out. Opportunities for choices occur any time an organization is expected to produce a decision (e.g. when contracts must be signed or money must be spent).

The decisions come about by *resolution*, by *oversight*, or by *flight*. If by resolution, then the choice resolves the problem, though this is likely to take time. If by oversight, the choice is made quickly, incidentally to other choices being made. If by flight, the original problem has gone (flown) away, leaving a choice which can now be readily made but solves nothing. Probably most decisions are made by oversight or flight, not by resolution.

Whether or not a decision happens is due to the 'temporal proximity' of what streams into the garbage can. That is, a decision happens when suitable problems, solutions, participants and choices coincide. When they do, solutions are attached to problems and problems to choices by participants who happen to have the time and energy to do it. So the decision that is made may be more or less 'uncoupled' from the apparent process of making it, being due to other coincidental reasons.

Seen like this, 'an organization is a collection of choices looking for problems, issues and feelings looking for decision situations in which they might be aired, solutions looking for issues to which they might be the answer, and decision-makers looking for work'. Though this may be so anywhere, nowhere is it more so than in an organized anarchy such as a university.

March admits that the picture may be overdrawn, but contends it is real enough to mean that the rational 'technology of reason' should be supplemented with a 'technology of foolishness'. Sometimes people *should* act *before* they think, so that they may discover new goals in the course of that action. They *should* make decisions with consequences for the future, in the knowledge that they do not know what will be wanted in the future. In terms of ostensible rationality, this is foolish. But decision-making needs scope for foolishness. Playfulness allows this. Playfulness is a deliberate (but temporary) suspension of the normal rational rules so that we can experiment. We need to play with foolish alternatives and *in*consistent possibilities. We need to treat goals as hypotheses to be changed, intuitions as real, hypocrisy as a transitional inconsistency, memory as an enemy of novelty, and experience not as fixed history but as a theory of what happened which we can change if that helps us to learn. From time to time we should be foolishly playful inside our garbage cans.

BIBLIOGRAPHY

CYERT, R. M., and MARCH, J. G., *A Behavioural Theory of the Firm*, Prentice-Hall, 1963.

MARCH, J. G., and OLSEN, J. P., *Ambiguity and Choice in Organizations*, Universitetsforlaget (Bergen, Norway), 1976.

MARCH, J. G., *Decisions and Organizations*, Blackwell, 1988.

Charles E. Lindblom

Charles Lindblom has long been Professor of Economics and Political Science at Yale University, and is a former director of the Yale Institution for Social and Policy Studies. He has served in a wide variety of academic and political posts including those of Guggenheim Fellow and economic adviser to the U S Aid Mission to India.

Lindblom asks how decisions should be made, and how they *are* made. His description and explanation of how they are made is framed primarily in terms of public administration and political systems, but it penetrates all forms of organizations. How do administrators and managers, indeed all who have to face substantial decisions, go about it? By root or by branch?

Lindblom supposes an instance of public policy. An administrator has to formulate policy with respect to inflation (this could as easily be a marketing director formulating a firm's pricing policy). To go to the root of the matter, one should attempt to list all possible variables however many there might be, such as full employment, reasonable business profits, protection of savings, stable exchange rates and so on. Then one should attempt to calculate how much a change on each of the variables is worth in terms of a change on each of the others. This done, the administrator can try to evaluate the alternative outcomes of the virtually infinitely large number of combinations that are possible. To do this would require gathering prodigious amounts of information. It would also require reconsideration of fundamentals of theory, from total central planning on the one hand to a completely free market on the other. The information and the alternatives, if ever they could be fully amassed, would be beyond comprehension.

Or instead the administrator could remain content with the comparatively simple goal of a period of stable prices. In this case most of the social values may be disregarded and attention given only to what is directly and immediately relevant. One would compare only a limited range of alternatives, most already familiar from previous occasions, and avoid recourse to theory or fundamental questioning. One could then make a decision which would have some partial success for a time.

The first approach to a policy decision described above aspires to the *rational deductive ideal*. This requires that all values be ascertained and be stated precisely enough for them to be arranged in order of priority, that principles then be derived which would indicate what information is necessary for every possible policy alternative to be compared with every other, that full information on each be obtained, and that logical calculative deduction then lead to the best alternative. This is an ideal of science, the complete deductive system, transferred to the field of values and application. On the face of it, it corresponds to good-sense notions of care and comprehensiveness. Its contemporary techniques are operations research, systems analysis, PPB (Planning-Programming-Budgeting) and the like. If followed, it would produce a *synoptic approach* to decision-making.

Yet it is difficult to find examples of this synoptic approach. Its advocates cannot point to where it is done. It is more an ideal than something actually accomplished; for it fails to adapt to what are in reality the troublesome characteristics of decisions, decision-makers, and decision-making.

Decision-makers need a way of deciding that takes account of these characteristics. They face situations in which the sheer multiplicity of values, and differences in formulating them, prevent their being exhaustively listed. Indeed, if any such attempt at listing were made, values and priorities would be changing whilst it was being done. It would be endless. In any case, because of the different partisan interests in any decision, decision-making has to proceed by 'mutual partisan adjustment', and so has to accommodate (but not necessarily reconcile) the many values of differing interests and cannot rank one above the other in explicit priority.

Decision-makers also need a way of deciding that is adapted to their own limited problem-solving capacities (see Simon p. 119). Mentally they could not cope with the deluge of information and alternatives implied in the synoptic approach. As Lindblom puts it, 'the mind flees from comprehensiveness'. In practice, their mental capacities are unlikely to be so stretched, for usually information is incomplete and inadequate, if only because the cost of finding out everything there is to know would be insupportable. Further, the presumption that what there is to know is finite and can be found out also presumes that facts and values occupy separate compartments, whereas in actuality they do not for they are inseparable. Different facts draw attention to different values, and values reinterpret facts. Likewise, the systems of variables with which decision-makers have to contend cannot be closed off to allow the finite analysis demanded by the synoptic approach, for there are always further interactions in fluid and open systems. Problems arise and extend in many forms.

So the strategy for making decisions that is commonly used by analysts and decision-makers is not synoptic. Lindblom terms what they do the *strategy of disjointed incrementalism*, a way of proceeding by *successive limited comparisons* that is far removed from the synoptic approach required by the rational deductive ideal.

Although disjointed incrementalism cannot be the only set of adaptations used to deal with the practical difficulties of decision-making, Lindblom suggests that it is the most prevalent. It makes changes in small increments by disjointed or uncoordinated processes (an increment is 'a small change in an important variable', but there is no sharp line between the incremental and the non-incremental which is a matter of degree along a continuum). It makes an indefinite, and apparently disorderly, series of small moves away from the ills of the day rather than towards defined goals. It leaves many aspects of problems seemingly unattended.

In summary, disjointed incrementalism is *incremental*, *restricted*, *means-oriented*, *reconstructive*, *serial*, *remedial* and *fragmented.*

Instead of rationally rooting out all the possibilities, the analyst or decision-maker simplifies the problem by contemplating only the margins by which circumstances might – if altered – differ. Marginal and therefore comprehendable change is examined and only a restricted number of alternatives are considered. Furthermore, the task is made manageable by considering only a restricted number of consequences for each alternative. The more remote or imponderable possibilities are left aside even if they are important, for to include them might prevent any decision being made at all.

While the conventional view is that means are adjusted to ends, the comparatively means-oriented strategy of disjointed incrementalism accepts the reverse. Ends are adjusted to means. This works both ways in a reciprocal relationship. Thus if the cost of the means of attaining the objective increases, either other means can be found, or the end objective can be changed so that it is brought within the means. Objectives can be fitted to policies as much as policies to objectives. This merges into the strategy's fourth feature, its active reconstructive response. Information is revised and reinterpreted, proposals are redesigned, and values are modified, continually. As problems are examined they are transformed.

The strategy's serial procedure is evident in its long chains of policy steps. There are never ending series of attacks on more or less permanent (though perhaps slowly changing) problems. These problems are rarely 'solved', only alleviated. The decision-maker does not look for some elusive 'solution', but looks instead for appropriate moves in a series that is expected to continue. The strategy therefore has a remedial orientation that identifies situations or ills from which to move *away*, rather than goals to move *towards*. Improvements here and there are preferred to grand aims.

Finally, disjointed incrementalism is fragmented by the way analysis and evaluation go ahead at different times, or at the same time, in many places. In the political sphere, a government policy may be under study at various times in several government departments and agencies, in universities, and in private firms and institutions (just as the policy of a single firm, for example, may be looked at by several of its departments, by its major customer, and by its bankers). Whereas the synoptic approach would try to rationally coordinate these efforts, disjointed incrementalism accepts their lack of coherence in return for the advantage of diversity. One may find what another misses. An overly controlled approach could 'coordinate out of sight' a potentially useful variety of contributions.

In these several ways the strategy of disjointed incrementalism scales problems down to size. It limits information, restricts choices and shortens horizons so that something can be done. What is overlooked now can be dealt with later. The strategy recognizes diverse values, but discourages intransigence by those involved because its reconstructive nature avoids rules or principles which, if defined, provoke firm stands by different parties.

The result is what Lindblom has called the *science of muddling through* – a practical and sophisticated adaptation to the impossibility of attaining the synoptic ideal. As he says, administrators often feel more confident when flying by the seat of their pants than when trying to follow the advice of theorists. Disjointed incrementalism is a working strategy and not merely a failure of synoptic method. It has the virtues of its own defects, which carry it pragmatically through.

On the face of it, the strategy looks conservative. It attempts small changes which do not have far-reaching consequences. Yet radical changes may be needed. However, Lindblom points out that it is logically possible to make changes as quickly by small frequent steps as it might be by more drastic and therefore less frequent steps. Each incremental step may be relatively easy, because it is not fraught with major consequences, and at least it is a step that can be taken, whereas the enormity of a fully synoptic consideration can deter decision-makers from even making a beginning, so that it achieves no movement at all.

BIBLIOGRAPHY

LINDBLOM, C. E., 'The Science of Muddling Through', *Public Administration Review* 19 (1959), 79–88; reprinted in D S. Pugh (ed.), *Organization Theory*, Penguin, 1990.

LINDBLOM, C. E., *The Policy-Making Process*, Prentice-Hall, 1968.

LINDBLOM, C. E., and BRAYBROOKE, D., *A Strategy of Decision*, Free Press, 1963.

LINDBLOM, C. E., and COHEN, D. K., *Usable Knowledge: Social Science and Social Problem Solving*, Yale University Press, 1979.

Victor H. Vroom

Victor Vroom has been involved for many years in research, teaching and consulting on the psychological analysis of behaviour in organizations. A Canadian by birth, he has been at McGill University, a number of US universities and is currently Searle Professor of Organization and Management, and Professor of Psychology at Yale University. His interests in the effects of personality on participation in decision-making began early and his doctoral dissertation on this topic won him the Ford Foundation Doctoral Dissertation Competition in 1959. He has also won the McKinsey Foundation Research Design Competition and the J. M. Cattell award of the American Psychological Association.

Vroom's dissertation corroborated previous findings that participation in decision-making has positive effects on attitudes and motivation. But in addition it showed that the size of these effects was a function of certain personality characteristics of the participants. Authoritarians and persons with weak independence needs are unaffected by the opportunity to participate; whereas equalitarians and those with strong independence needs develop more positive attitudes and greater motivation for effective performance through participation. The study did point out that there are a number of different processes related to participation which might be affected differently.

Much more recently Vroom (in collaboration with P. W. Yetton and A. G. Jago) has explored in much greater depth the processes of management decision-making and the variations in subordinate participation which can come about. Possible decision processes which a manager might use in dealing with an issue affecting a group of subordinates are as follows (though there are some variations if the issue concerns one subordinate only):

AI You solve the problem or make the decision yourself, using information available to you at that time.

AII You obtain the necessary information from your subordinate(s), then decide on the solution to the problem yourself. You may or may not tell your subordinates what the problem is when getting the information from them. The role played by your subordinates in making the decision is clearly one of providing necessary information to you, rather than generating or evaluating alternative solutions.

CI You share the problem with relevant subordinates individually, getting their ideas and suggestions without bringing them together as a group. Then *you* make the decisions that may or may not reflect your subordinates' influence.

CII You share the problem with your subordinates as a group, collectively obtaining their ideas and suggestions. Then *you* make the decision that may or may not reflect your subordinates' influence.

GII You share a problem with your subordinates as a group. Together you generate and evaluate alternatives and attempt to reach agreement (consensus) on a solution. Your role is much like that of chairman. You do not try to influence the group to adopt 'your' solution and you are willing to accept and implement any solution that has the support of the entire group.

Processes AI and AII are designated autocratic processes, CI and CII consultative processes, and GII is a group process. (GI applies to single subordinate issues.) Having identified these processes Vroom and Yetton's research programme then proceeded to answer two basic questions:

1. What decision-making processes *should* managers use to deal effectively with the problems they encounter in their jobs? This is a normative or prescriptive question. To answer it would require setting up a logical 'model' with a series of steps or procedures by which managers could rationally determine which was the most effective process to inaugurate.
2. What decision-making processes *do* managers use in dealing with their problems and what factors affect their choice of processes and degree of subordinate participation? This is a descriptive question, and the answer is important in delineating how far away from a rational approach managers are in their decision-making. We could then ask what activities of training or development could lead managers to a more effective decision-making style.

It is in their answer to the first question that Vroom and his collaborators have made a most distinctive contribution. They have developed a detailed normative model of decision-making processes based on rational principles consistent with existing evidence on the consequences of participation for organizational effectiveness. They begin by distinguishing three classes of consequences which influence decision effectiveness:

1. The quality or rationality of the decision – clearly a process which jeopardized this would be ineffective.
2. The acceptance or commitment on the part of the subordinates to execute the decision effectively – if this commitment is necessary then processes which do not generate it even though they give a high quality decision would be ineffective.
3. The amount of time required to make the decision – a decision process which took less time, if it were equally effective, would normally be preferable to one which took longer.

These consequences generate a set of rules for the model which may then be applied to the characteristics of a manager's problem under consideration. The model will then indicate which of the decision processes is appropriate to the particular case. The model can be expressed in the form of a decision tree as shown on page 136. In the Decision Model, the problem characteristics are presented as questions. The manager starts at the left-hand side and moves to the right along the path determined by the answer to the question above each box. At the final point of the line the model shows which of the decision processes should be used to reach, in the least time, a quality decision which will be found acceptable.

As will be seen from the Decision Model, all decision processes (autocratic, consultative, group) are applicable in some circumstances and how often each should be used will depend on the type of decisions that the manager has to take. The normative model requires that all managers, if they are to be rational and effective, have to be able to operate across the whole range. In later work Vroom and Jago have elaborated the model to give greater discrimination among options and thus allow more detailed and more effective targeting of the decision process to the manager's problem. They have also made the more elaborate model available for use via a computer program.

The research undertaken by Vroom and his collaborators to answer their second question – how do managers actually behave? – is based on two methods. In the first, many managers were asked to recall decision problems and how they tackled them in terms of the questions of the Decision Model. The second method involved many managers assessing a set of standardized problem descriptions and giving their preferred solutions.

The most striking finding of these descriptive studies was that, while there were certainly average differences between managers in their use of various decision processes, these were small in comparison with the *range* of processes used by any individual manager. No managers indicated that they would use the same process on all decisions and most

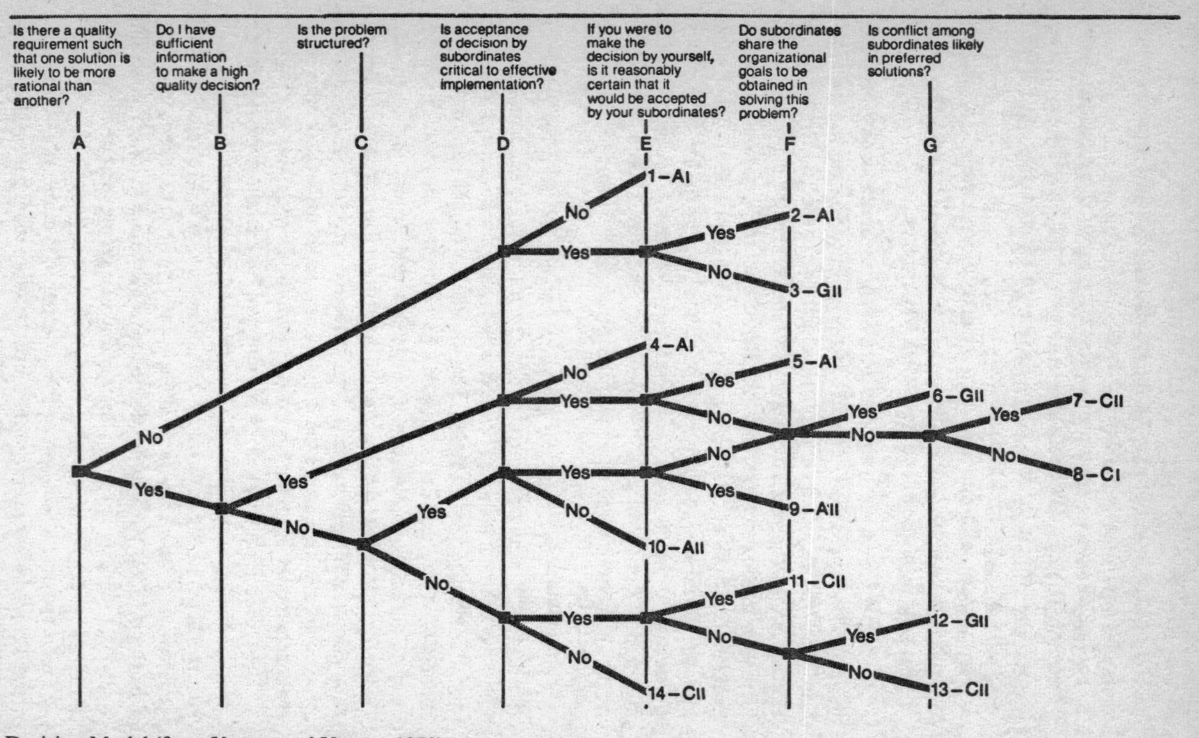

Decision Model (from Vroom and Yetton, 1973).

used all five of the decision processes above under some circumstances. 'It makes more sense to talk about participative and autocratic situations than it does to talk about participative and autocratic managers.'

The descriptive research also enabled a comparison of what managers do (or say they would do) and what the model would designate as rational behaviour. On average, a 'typical' manager was found to use the same decision process as that required by the Decision Model in 40 per cent of the situations. In a further quarter of the situations they used a process which is called 'feasible' in that it satisfied the constraints of the model on protecting decision quality and acceptability but it would not be the least time-consuming. Only in about one third of the situations did the typical manager initiate a process which will risk quality or acceptability. In addition it was found that the constraints necessary to achieve acceptability were much more frequently ignored than those necessary to achieve quality.

Vroom has designed a leadership development programme based on his normative model which will enable managers to analyse their own decision processes against that of the model and see where they depart from the rational constraints for effective decision-making. The model proposes far greater variation for each problem situation than the typical manager exhibits. Using the model as a basis for making decisions would require such a manager to become both more autocratic *and* more participative according to the problem (cf. Fiedler, p. 181, for an opposing view on this issue).

BIBLIOGRAPHY

VROOM, V. H., *Some Personality Determinants of the Effects of Participation*, Prentice-Hall, 1960.

VROOM, V. H., A New Look at Managerial Decision Making', *Organizational Dynamics 5*, 1974, 66–80; reprinted in D. S. Pugh (ed.), *Organization Theory*, Penguin Books, 1990.

VROOM, V. H., and YETTON, P. W., *Leadership and Decision-making*, University of Pittsburgh Press, 1973.

VROOM, V. H., and JAGO, A. G., *The New Leadership: Managing Participation in Organizations*, Prentice-Hall, 1988.

Michel Crozier

The distinctly French view of organizations contributed by Michel Crozier arises both from his French birth and experience and from the many periods he has spent in the United States. These periods away from France give him a perspective on his own society. He is Director of the Centre for the Sociology of Organizations in Paris, under the auspices of the Centre National de la Recherche Scientifique (CNRS), and has a long record of research in France. This has covered a wide range of organizations and administrative and social problems, but with an emphasis on studies of public administration and state-owned industries. However, his early training in sociology was in the United States, and he has spent many subsequent periods at Stanford and Harvard.

Although Crozier's view has its origins in research in France, it penetrates bureaucracies everywhere. He does not see them as monolithic rational structures, but as systems in which, despite all efforts at control, individuals and groups of individuals have room for manoeuvre. There is a constant interaction between the system and the actors in the system.

This view is distinctively founded on the concept of the power *game*. An organization is seen as a series of enmeshed power games, an 'ensemble' of games. This idea is no mere colourful image. Games are very real to those in organizations. Indeed, an organization is not so much the direct creation of deliberate design as the result of the ensemble of games. The game channels power relationships and enables cooperation, reconciling the freedom of those in the organization with the constraints it places upon them.

Games are played between groups of partners of many kinds, for example between superiors and subordinates such as managers and workers, or between departments and sections. The players evolve different strategies which govern what they do. Superiors may follow a strategy of 'divide and rule'; subordinates may follow a defensive strategy to protect whatever scope they may have to do things in their own way, free of interference from bosses or new regulations; occupational groups such as maintenance engineers may follow conservative (or aggressive) strategies toward technical modernization, and so on. Crozier calls this a *strategic model* of organization.

Players go so far but not too far in pursuing their strategies. While all are free to gain whatever advantage can be got from a strategy rationally designed to serve their interests, the continuance of the organization is necessary for them to be able to play at all. These are not life-and-death struggles but games for position within a system, therefore limits are accepted. These are the rules of the game which players in each game must respect if it is to continue. They are not formally set-down rules, but principles which can be discovered by analysing the players' recurrent behaviour, in the same way as their strategies can be seen in what they do. There may not be complete consensus on the rules, and some players may be endeavouring to change them, but they are sufficiently acknowledged and persistent for newcomers to learn them and to absorb the associated norms and values which define acceptable and unacceptable strategies.

The players in a game are far from equal – some are more powerful than others – and their roles differ further between games, so that players who are powerful in one game may be weak in another. However, their strategies share a common fundamental objective – to gain whatever advantage is possible, within the constraining rules of the game, by restricting the choices of alternatives open to others while preserving or enhancing their own choices. The aim is to manoeuvre others into positions where their actions can be determined, while retaining one's own freedom of action. All attempt to defend and extend their own discretion and to limit their dependence, while placing others in the reverse position.

The most revealing case among those described by Crozier is that of the maintenance workers in what he terms the 'Industrial Monopoly', the French nationalized tobacco industry. At the time of Crozier's research, at the end of the 1950s and beginning of the 1960s, this was dispersed throughout the country in a large number of small and very similar factories. Each employed in the order of 350 to 400 people of which perhaps one third were direct production workers. These workers were women, and their job was to operate the semi-automatic machines turning out cigarettes, etc.

The organization was very stable, and each small factory worked in a controlled environment. Finance, raw material procurement, distribution and sales were all centrally controlled from Paris, so each local plant could get on with its task of production, unimpeded by problems. Except one. Machine stoppages.

These stoppages occurred because of breakdowns and because of variations in the tobacco leaf which required constant adjustment of machines. They were the only major happenings that could not be dealt with by impersonal bureaucratic rules or bureaucratic actions from Paris. Yet if machines stopped, work stopped, and the factory stopped making what it was there for. Who could do something about it? Only the dozen or so male maintenance workers under the factory's technical engineer, who alone knew how to set and to repair the machines. No bureaucrat in Paris, no local factory director, not even the production workers on the machines, knew what they knew. They acquired the tricks of their trade from one another, and kept them to themselves. They did not explain what they did to anyone else. In their eyes it was an unforgivable sin for a production worker herself to 'fool around' with her machine which she should not touch beyond operating it in the normal way. Thus the maintenance workers succeeded in making the production workers directly, and everyone else indirectly, dependent upon them. All the others were constrained by the maintenance workers being the only ones able to deal with stoppages, whilst the maintenance workers themselves preserved their freedom of choice over what to do.

They could do so because they were powerful; and they were powerful because of their 'control over the last source of uncertainty remaining in a completely routinized organizational system'. Machine stoppages occurred unpredictably and theirs was the choice of what to do. This gave them power because those who face and cope with uncertainties have power over others who are dependent upon their choices. In the long run, power is closely related to those uncertainties on which the life of an organization depends, and the strategies of the groups in the power games are aimed at controlling the 'ultimate strategic sources of uncertainties'. *Uncertainty explains power.*

The maintenance workers therefore had power because whilst everything else was under bureaucratic control the uncertain machine stoppages were not. These had to be dealt with on the spot as they happened. They presented the maintenance workers with an opportunity which was conspicuous because it was the sole uncertainty in each factory. In other organizations the sources of uncertainty may not be so conspicuous, but in all organizations they come and go and as they do so the power of those who confront them waxes and wanes. Maintenance workers are only one example: the same applies to the rise and fall of financial experts, of production control specialists, and so on.

Why is it then that powerful experts are not able to cling to power indefinitely? If the uncertainty continues and with it their know-how they could indeed keep their grip on power, but this is unlikely because their success is self-defeating. The rationalization inherent in organizations breeds constant attempts to bring areas of uncertainty within the range of formal controls, and experts are themselves agents of the rationalization that diminishes their own power. The more they succeed in recording their own know-how in bureaucratic procedures and regulations, the more their own power to deal with the uncertainties themselves is curtailed. Their choices become restricted. Therefore the maintenance workers in the tobacco factories strove to keep their rules of thumb to themselves and to prevent them becoming bureaucratized. Even though there were officially laid down instructions for the setting and maintenance of machines kept at head office in Paris, these were completely disregarded by the maintenance workers and there were no copies in the factories themselves. For *the routinization of uncertainty removes power.*

This shapes strategies up and down hierarchies as well as between occupational groupings. The battle between superiors and subordinates involves a basic strategy by which subordinates resist rules which encroach upon their discretion, whilst pressing for rules which will limit the discretion of their superiors over them.

It is possible for opposed strategies to interlock in a series of bureaucratic vicious circles which block change. Administrators try to extend bureaucratic regulation: those subjected to it resist. The directors of the tobacco factories typically pressed for the modernization of procedures, whilst the technical engineers resisted anything that might alter the position of their maintenance workers. Crozier sees French society as a whole as an example of this, for its tendencies to bureaucratic centralization and impersonality provoke protective strategies by those affected, and these strategies in turn provoke greater bureaucratization. In every branch of administration each level of hierarchy becomes a layer protected from those above and beneath. Those beneath restrict communication to those above and stall any threatening changes, while those above make ill-informed decisions which are not carried out as intended but from the consequences of which they are shielded.

This gives rise to a peculiar rhythm of change in bureaucratic organizations, certainly in France and perhaps elsewhere too. It is an alternation of long periods of stability with very short periods of crisis and change. Conflicts are stifled until they explode. Explosive crises are therefore endemic to such bureaucracies, and necessary to them as a means for change. At such times in French bureaucracies, personal authority supersedes the rules as someone is able to force some change out of the crisis. *Authoritarian reformer figures* wait amid the bureaucratic routine for that moment of crisis when the system will need them.

Yet Crozier is optimistic. He hopes that if reforms were made in training and recruitment for French public administration, and in its caste system, the elites could be opened up. He argues that the large organizations of the modern world are not necessarily inimical to change, for change has never been faster and it is fastest in those societies with the largest organizations. But there is always a risk that bureaucratic structures lead to forms of power game which block the changes that are needed.

BIBLIOGRAPHY

CROZIER, M., *The Bureaucratic Phenomenon*, Tavistock Publications and University of Chicago Press, 1964.

CROZIER, M., and FRIEDBERG, E., *Actors and Systems*, University of Chicago Press, 1980.

CROZIER, M., 'Comparing Structures and Comparing Games' in G. Hofstede and S. Kassim (eds.), *European Contributions to Organization Theory*, Van Gorcum, 1976; reprinted in D. S. Pugh (ed.), *Organization Theory*, Penguin, 1984.

Arnold S. Tannenbaum

Arnold Tannenbaum did not begin as the social psychologist he later became. His first degree was in electrical engineering from Purdue University. He went on to take his Ph.D. at Syracuse University, and to join the staff of one of the leading and longest established American social science institutes, the Institute for Social Research not far from Detroit, where he has worked ever since as researcher, teacher and consultant. He is both a Program Director in the Institute's Survey Research Center and Professor in the Department of Psychology at the University of Michigan.

In the small text he published in 1966, Tannenbaum set out clearly the view of organizational functioning that has shaped his work for many years. 'Hierarchy is divisive, it creates resentment, hostility and opposition. Participation reduces disaffection and increases the identification of members with the organization.' What is more: 'Paradoxically, through participation, management increases its control by giving up some of its authority.'

Early in his research career, Tannenbaum found that in trade unions the more effective and active local branches had both more influential officers and more influential members, at first sight an impossibility. An impossibility, that is, if control of an organization was thought of as a given quantity, something to be divided so that if someone had more then someone else had less; but not impossible if control of an organization was expandable so that everyone could have more. It is this possibility that shapes Tannenbaum's view of what organizations can be.

His work has focused on control, for organizations are means whereby the behaviour of large numbers of individuals is controlled. That is, people have to work together more or less as they are intended to if the aims of the organizations are to be achieved, whether that organization is a trade union, a firm, a welfare agency, a cooperative or an Israeli kibbutz, a financial institution, a brokerage firm, or a branch of the American League of Women Voters – all examples of organizations which Tannenbaum and his colleagues or others following their lead have studied. Control is any process by which a person or group of persons determines (i.e. 'intentionally affects') the behaviour of another person or group, in other words, causes someone else to do what they want them to do. In an organization this may be by orders or by persuasion, by threats or by promises, through written communications or through discussion, even indirectly by fixing the speed of a machine that someone else must keep up with or by programming a computer to produce information they must deal with – or by any other means having such an effect.

The way of representing control used in studies by Tannenbaum and his colleagues over many years is to ask members of organizations how much influence they and others have. They are asked a question worded typically as follows: 'How much say or influence does each of the following groups have over what goes on (in the organization)?' The groups referred to are hierarchical echelons such as managers, supervisors, and workers; the groupings can be varied as appropriate. This simple question is capable of yielding a great amount of information since even with only three groups – managers, supervisors and workers – those in each group can rate the influence of both the other two groups and of themselves, so that a large number of cross-checking ratings are obtained. If four, five or six groupings are used the information is greater again. The wording of the question can also be varied to refer more specifically to the influence over what others do or over policy, for example.

Members of organizations respond to the question by ticking one of five categories for each group, in the form:

	Little or no influence	*Some influence*	*Quite a bit of influence*	*A great deal of influence*	*A very great deal of influence*
Managers	—	—	—	—	—
Supervisors	—	—	—	—	—
Workers	—	—	—	—	—

The degrees of influence are scored from one to five so that a tick under 'Little' scores one, a tick under 'Some' scores two, and so on with 'A very great deal' scoring five.

Responding to such a question in this way gives a representation of how actual influence is perceived by those involved. A second and equally large amount of information is obtained by asking the same question again but with the word 'does' replaced by 'should'. This gives preferred or ideal influence.

The impact of Tannenbaum's work, and its interpretation, are heightened by the way in which the results can be portrayed. They can be plotted on what are called control graphs. Various different averagings of scores can be plotted, but usually the influence ratings given to each group by all the others and by itself are added and its mean score is calculated. In the example above, this would give a mean score out of five for managers, another for supervisors, and another for workers, which could then be plotted on a control graph in which the three hierarchical groups were placed evenly along the lateral axis in hierarchical order. A simplified but not unrepresentative hypothetical result might look like the graph below.

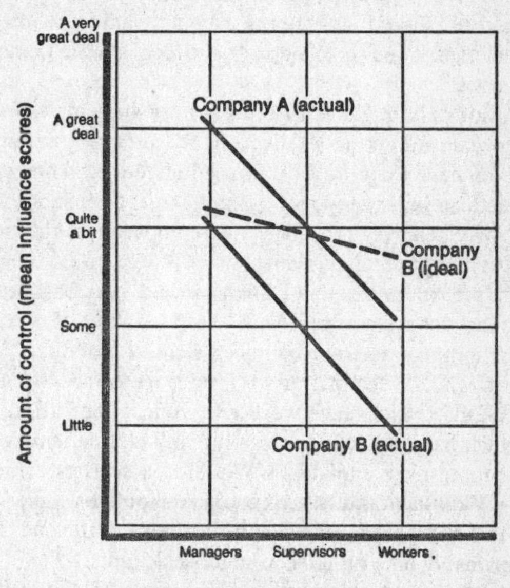

The lines are drawn through the three graph points for the mean scores for each group (managers, workers, supervisors) on the vertical control (influence score) axis.

The immediate visual impact of a control graph is from the *slope* of the lines, its most obvious if not necessarily most significant feature. In the graph, the two solid lines represent the actual (as against ideal) distributions of control in two hypothetical companies. Tannenbaum interprets such left to right slopes as showing a hierarchical distribution in which there is a sharp reduction in control from one level to the next down the hierarchy. Companies A and B show in their actual hierarchies of control the classical view of the industrial firm. Tannenbaum finds that in practically all manufacturing organizations in Western industrialized nations, all the employees whether bosses or subordinates report the steeply graded hierarchy that he sees as divisive, and fraught with resentment and hostility.

This may be unavoidable in large-scale manufacturing, and even ideal slopes (plots of the responses to the 'should' question) do not fundamentally challenge the basic hierarchy of control. No one in manufacturing organizations suggests anything other than that upper levels should have more control than lower levels – the slope does not flatten out nor tip the other way – but the *degree* of differentiation *is* challenged. The ideal slope is often less steep. Lower level employees frequently feel that they themselves should have more say in what goes on, as in the hypothetical ideal slope for Company B which is more democratic than the actual slope.

Further, not only might the steeply graded hierarchies in large-scale industrial organizations be levelled out to some degree, but it is also possible to manage them in ways that mitigate the hierarchy's negative effects. American supervisors, for example, treat their subordinates more as equals, with relative informality, as compared to the typical authoritarian approach in Italian plants.

Tannenbaum recognizes that Italian workers may be more concerned with changing the system than with the possibility of working better. Certainly a nation's socio-economic system is embodied in forms of organization which affect hierarchy. The slope of control graphs from Yugoslav plants (which have workers' councils) and from Israeli kibbutzim (which have collective ownership and elected managers) are not as steep as those from capitalistic Western enterprises, which is not to say that the Yugoslavs and Israelis could or should be copied everywhere else, for Yugoslav managers can be authoritarian, and the kibbutz system is probably only possible in small-scale units.

The type of membership that is appropriate to the purpose of the organization also affects control. In organizations that depend on a voluntary membership (such as American trade unions and the American League of Women Voters) the rank and file exert much greater influence than do the paid employees in industry; and similar results in Brazilian development banks staffed by highly educated professionals suggest that professionalization has the same effect because these members are relied on to do their work with less direct control, and more attention is paid to their views.

However, though the slope of the line in a control graph is its most instantly obvious feature, it does not in Tannenbaum's view depict the most important feature of an organization which, he says, is the *total control* within an organization, as depicted on the graph by the *area* beneath the line. In the graph both companies have identical hierarchical slopes but the line for Company A is higher than that for Company B, so the area beneath the line for Company A (i.e. between the line and the lateral axis at the base of the graph) is greater. In other words, the influence scores for all groups are greater, so that everyone has more control. Here is the visual representation of the apparent paradox that lower level employees such as workers can have greater control and yet not detract from the control exercised by managers. Indeed, managers too may then have greater control. This is possible because the total amount of influence, the size of the 'influence pie', can be expanded – and can be greater in one organization than in another because control is not a 'zero-sum' process.

The reason for this is that the leaders are also the led. Superiors depend upon their subordinates to get things done. Authoritarian bosses who take a zero-sum view assume a fixed amount of total control and cling to what they perceive as their rightful major share of it. They may look as if they are dominating everyone but their actual influence on what others do may be very little. Subordinates in this situation will also take a zero-sum view and will defend their share from encroachment. Conflict and minimal cooperation are likely to result. If superiors assume an expandable amount of total control, they can communicate readily with subordinates, welcome opinions, and take up suggestions; in other words, invite influence over themselves. At the same time, the involvement of subordinates in what is being done means that the superiors' influence expands also, for they are more likely to do what needs to be done.

Research results show that a greater amount of control exists in Japanese mining and manufacturing companies compared with American equivalent organizations. 'Progressive' dioceses in the Roman Catholic church (i.e. those where the bishop is rated as positive to democratizing decision-making) have more total control than conservative ones, as do plants incorporating self-managing sociotechnical groups (see Trist p. 186) compared with conventional factories.

Greater effectiveness of an organization, in terms of morale and productivity, is likely to be linked more to increasing the total amount of control than to democratizing its hierarchical distribution, because all concerned are more fully controlled and in control through interlocking influence. This is true as much of privately owned American firms as it is of collectively owned Israeli kibbutzim.

Tannenbaum's research challenges the commonplace view that control is and should be unilateral, from the leaders to the led. Leaders have greater control when the led also have greater control. Though diminishing the slope of hierarchies can be important, too much attention is paid to this 'power equalization' and too little to the possibilities of expanding the total. The evidence suggests that people are more interested in exercising more control themselves than in exactly how much others may have.

The strength of Tannenbaum's challenging perspective is that it is based on a uniquely sustained series of research projects in many countries, using standard methods, which have confirmed the results again and again.

BIBLIOGRAPHY

TANNENBAUM, A. S., *Social Psychology of the Work Organization*, Wadsworth (California) and Tavistock, 1966.

TANNENBAUM, A. S., *Control in Organizations*, McGraw-Hill, 1968.

TANNENBAUM, A. S., KAVCIC, B., ROSNER, M., VIANELLO, M., and WIESER, G., *Hierarchy in Organizations*, Jossey-Bass, 1974.

TANNENBAUM, A. S., 'Controversies about Control and Democracy in Organizations', in R. N. Stern and S. McCarthy (eds.), *The International Yearbook of Organizational Democracy, Vol III*, Wiley, 1986.

5 People in Organizations

Management succeeds or fails in proportion as it is accepted without reservation by the group as authority and leader.
ELTON MAYO

The entire organization must consist of a multiple overlapping group structure with *every* work group using group decision-making processes skilfully.
RENSIS LIKERT

The average human being learns, under proper conditions, not only to accept but to seek responsibility.
DOUGLAS MCGREGOR

The 9, 9 orientation to the management of production and people aims at integrating these two aspects of work under conditions of high concern for both.
ROBERT R. BLAKE and JANE S. MOUTON

It is my hypothesis that the present organizational strategies developed and used by administrators (be they industrial, educational, religious, governmental or trade union) lead to human and organizational decay. It is also my hypothesis that this need not be so.
CHRIS ARGYRIS

The successful manager must be a good diagnostician and must value a spirit of enquiry.
EDGAR H. SCHEIN

The primary functions of any organization, whether religious, political or industrial, should be to implement the needs of man to enjoy a meaningful existence.
FREDERICK HERZBERG

The closest approximation to the all round good leader is likely to be the individual who intuitively or through training knows how to manage his environment so that the leadership situation best matches his leadership style.
FRED E. FIEDLER

Only organizations based on the redundancy of functions (as opposed to the redundancy of parts) have the flexibility and innovative potential to give the possibility of adaptation to a rapid change rate, increasing complexity and environmental uncertainty.
ERIC TRIST

By beginning from, and attempting to make sense of, the definitions of the situation held by the actors, the Action perspective provides a means of understanding the range of reactions to apparently 'identical' social situations.
DAVID SILVERMAN

Organizations are systems of interdependent *human beings*. Although this has been recognized implicitly by the writers of the previous sections, and explicitly by some, their main concern has been with the 'formal system' – its aims, the principles on which it should be constituted to achieve them, and the methods by which it should function. People have then been considered as one of the essential resources required to achieve the aims. But people are a rather special sort of resource. They not only work for the organization – they *are* the organization.

The behaviour of the members of an organization clearly affects both its structure and its functioning, as well as the principles on which it can be managed. Most importantly, human beings affect the aims of organizations in which they participate – not merely the methods used to accomplish them. The writers in this chapter are social scientists who are specifically concerned to analyse the behaviour of people and its effects on all aspects of the organization. They have studied human attitudes, expectations, value systems, tensions and conflicts and the effects these have on productivity, adaptability, cohesion and morale. They have regarded the organization as a 'natural system' – an organism whose processes have to be studied in their own right – rather than as a 'formal system' – a mechanism designed to achieve particular ends.

Elton Mayo is the founding father of the 'Human Relations Movement' which brought into prominence the view that workers and managers must first be understood as human beings. Rensis Likert and Douglas McGregor reject the underlying assumptions about human behaviour on which formal organizations have been built and propose new methods of management based on a more adequate understanding of human motivation, while Robert Blake and Jane Mouton describe a form of management which shows equal high concern for both production and people.

Chris Argyris has been concerned to examine and control the inevitable conflict between the needs of the individual and the management of organizations, and Edgar Schein to understand and manage the relationship between the individual's career and the organization's culture. Frederick Herzberg determines how people's characteristically human needs for growth and development may be satisfied in work.

Fred Fiedler analyses appropriate styles of leadership for effectiveness in differing situations. Eric Trist and his colleagues at the Tavistock Institute demonstrate the utility of designing groups and organizations to take account of human and social, as well as technical, concerns. In contrast David Silverman argues that the 'Action Frame of Reference' contributes more to our understanding of how people act in organizational life.

Elton Mayo and the Hawthorne Investigations

Elton Mayo (1880–1949) was an Australian who spent most of his working life at Harvard University, eventually becoming Professor of Industrial Research in the Graduate School of Business Administration. In this post he was responsible for the initiation and direction of many research projects, the most famous being the five-year investigation of the Hawthorne works of the Western Electric Company in Chicago. Immediately prior to his death, Mayo was consultant on industrial problems to the British Government.

Elton Mayo has often been called the founder of both the Human Relations movement and of industrial sociology. The research that he directed showed the importance of groups in affecting the behaviour of individuals at work and enabled him to make certain deductions about what managers ought to do.

Like most of his contemporaries, Mayo's initial interests were in fatigue, accidents and labour turnover, and the effect on these of rest pauses and physical conditions of work. One of his first investigations was of a spinning mill in Philadelphia where labour turnover in one department was 250 per cent compared with an average of 6 per cent for all the other departments. Rest pauses were introduced by Mayo and production and morale improved. When the operatives took part in fixing the frequency and duration of the pauses a further improvement was registered and morale in the whole factory also improved. At the end of the first year, turnover in the department concerned was down to the average for the rest of the mill. The initial explanation was that the rest pauses, in breaking up the monotony of the job, improved the mental and physical condition of the workers. However, after subsequent investigations, Mayo modified his explanation.

The major investigation which led to this modification and which laid the basis for a great many subsequent studies was the Hawthorne Experiment carried out between 1927 and 1932. Prior to the entry of Mayo's team an inquiry had been made by a number of engineers into the effect of illumination on workers and their work. Two groups of workers had been isolated and the lighting conditions for one had been varied and for the other held constant. No significant differences in output were found between the two; indeed whatever was done with the lighting, production rose in *both* groups.

At this point the Industrial Research team directed by Mayo took over. The first stage of their inquiry is known as the Relay Assembly Test Room. Six female operatives, engaged in assembling telephone relays, were segregated in order to observe the effect on output and morale of various changes in the conditions of work. During the five years of experiment various changes were introduced and a continuous record of output was kept. At first a special group payment scheme was introduced: previously the women had been grouped with one hundred other operatives for incentive payment purposes. Other changes introduced at various times were rest pauses in several different forms (varying in length and spacing), shorter hours and refreshments, in all more than ten changes. Before putting the changes into effect, the investigators spent a lot of time discussing them with the women. Communication between the workers and the research team was very full and open throughout the experimental period. Almost without exception output increased with each change made.

The next stage in the experiment was to return to the original conditions. The operatives reverted to a forty-eight-hour six-day week, no incentive, no rest pauses and no refreshment. Output went up to the highest yet recorded. By this time it had become clear, to quote Mayo, 'that the itemized changes experimentally imposed . . . could not be used to explain the major change – the continually increasing production'. The explanation eventually given was that the women experienced a tremendous increase in work satisfaction because they had greater freedom in their working environment and control over their own pace-setting. The six operatives had become a social group with their own standards and expectations. By removing the women from the normal setting of work and by intensifying their interaction and cooperation, informal practices, values, norms and social relationships had been built up giving the group high cohesion. Also, the communication system between the researchers and the workers was extremely effective; this meant that the norms of output were those that the women felt the researchers desired. The supervisors took a personal interest in each worker and showed pride in the record of the group. The result was that the workers and the supervisors developed a sense of participation and as a result established a completely new working pattern. Mayo's generalization was that work satisfaction depends to a large extent on the informal social pattern of the work group. Where norms of cooperativeness and high output are established because of a feeling of importance, physical conditions have little impact.

However, this is the explanation arrived at in later years. At the time of the actual experiment, the continually increasing output was regarded as something of a mystery so an inquiry was instituted into conditions in the factory at large. This took the form of an interview programme. It was quickly realized that such a programme told the researchers little about the actual conditions in the factory but a great deal about the attitudes of various employees. The major finding of this stage of the inquiry was that many problems of worker–management cooperation were the results of the emotionally based attitudes of the workers rather than of objective difficulties in the situation. Workers, thought Mayo, were activated by a 'logic of sentiment', whereas management is concerned with the 'logic of cost and efficiency'. Conflict is inevitable unless this difference is understood and provided for.

The third stage of the investigation was to observe a group performing a task in a natural setting, i.e. a non-experimental situation. A number of male employees in what became known as the Bank Wiring Observation Room were put under constant observation and their output recorded. It was found that they restricted their output; the group had a standard for output and this was not exceeded by any individual worker. The attitude of the members of the group towards the company's financial incentive scheme was one of indifference. The group was highly integrated with its own social structure and code of behaviour which clashed with that of management. Essentially this code was composed of solidarity on the part of the group against management. Not too much work should be done, that would be ratebusting; on the other hand, not too little work should be done, that would be chiselling. There was little recognition of the organization's formal allocation of roles. This was confirmation of the importance of informal social groupings in determining levels of output.

Taken as a whole, the significance of the Hawthorne investigation was in 'discovering' the informal organization which, it is now realized, exists in all organizations. It demonstrated the importance to individuals of stable social relationships in the work situation. It confirmed Mayo in his wider thinking that what he calls the 'rabble hypothesis' about human behaviour (that each individual pursues only a narrow rational self-interest) was completely false. It confirmed his view that the breakdown of traditional values in society could be countered by creating a situation in industry conducive to spontaneous cooperation.

For Mayo, one of the major tasks of management is to organize spontaneous cooperation, thereby preventing the further breakdown of society. As traditional attachments to community and family disappear, and as the workplace increases in importance, the support given by traditional institutions must now be given by the organization. Conflict, competition and disagreement between individuals are to be avoided by management understanding its role as providing the basis for group affiliation. From the end of the Hawthorne project to his death Mayo was interested in discovering how spontaneous cooperation could be achieved. It is this which has been the basis of the Human Relations movement – the use of the insights of the social sciences to secure the commitment of individuals to the ends and activities of the organization.

The impact of Hawthorne and Mayo on both management and academics has been tremendous. It led to a fuller realization and understanding of the 'human factor' in work situations. Central to this was the 'discovery' of the informal group as an outlet for the aspirations of the worker. His work also led to an emphasis on the importance of an adequate communication system, particularly upwards from workers to management. The investigation showed, to quote Mayo, that 'management succeeds or fails in proportion as it is accepted without reservation by the group as authority and leader'.

BIBLIOGRAPHY

MAYO, E., *The Human Problems of an Industrial Civilization*, Macmillan, 1933.

MAYO, E., *The Social Problems of an Industrial Civilization*, Routledge & Kegan Paul, 1949.

ROETHLISBERGER, F. J., and DICKSON, W. J., *Management and the Worker*, Harvard University Press, 1949.

Rensis Likert and Douglas McGregor

Rensis Likert (1903–1981) was an American social psychologist who in 1949 established the Institute of Social Research at the University of Michigan. Until his retirement in 1969, he was thus at the head of one of the major institutions conducting research into human behaviour in organizations. On his retirement he formed Rensis Likert Associates, a consulting firm, to put his ideas about the management of organizations into wider practice. His books are based on the numerous research studies which he and his colleagues have conducted. His last book was jointly written with his research collaborator and wife, Jane Gibson Likert.

Douglas McGregor (1906–1964) was a social psychologist who published a number of research papers in this field. For some years he was President (i.e. Chief Executive) of Antioch College and he has described how this period as a top administrator affected his views on organizational functioning. From 1954 until his death, he was Professor of Management at the Massachusetts Institute of Technology.

'Managers with the best records of performance in American business and government are in the process of pointing the way to an appreciably more effective system of management than now exists,' proclaims Likert. Research studies have shown that departments which are low in efficiency tend to be in the charge of supervisors who are 'job-centred'. That is they 'tend to concentrate on keeping their subordinates busily engaged in going through a specified work cycle in a prescribed way and at a satisfactory rate as determined by time standards'. This attitude is clearly derived from that of Taylor (see p. 90) with its emphasis on breaking down the job into component parts, selecting and training people to do them, and exerting constant pressure to achieve output. Supervisors see themselves as getting the job done with the resources (which includes the people) at their disposal.

Supervisors with the best record of performance are found to focus their attention on the human aspects of their subordinates' problems, and on building effective work groups which are set high achievement goals. These supervisors are 'employee-centred'. They regard their jobs as dealing with human beings rather than with the work; they attempt to know them as individuals. They see their function as helping them to do the job efficiently. They exercise general rather than detailed supervision, and are more concerned with targets than methods. They allow maximum participation in decision-making. If high performance is to be obtained, a supervisor must not only be employee-centred but must also have high performance goals and be capable of exercising the decision-making processes to achieve them.

In summarizing these findings, Likert distinguishes four systems of management. System 1 is the exploitive authoritative type where management uses fear and threats, communication is downward, superiors and subordinates are psychologically far apart, the bulk of decisions is taken at the top of the organization, etc. System 2 is the benevolent authoritative type where management uses rewards, subordinates' attitudes are subservient to superiors, information flowing upward is restricted to what the boss wants to hear, policy decisions are taken at the top but decisions within a prescribed framework may be delegated to lower levels, etc. System 3 is the consultative type where management uses rewards, occasional punishments and some involvement is sought; communication is both down and up but upward communication other than that which the boss wants to hear is given in limited amounts and only cautiously. In this system subordinates can have a moderate amount of influence on the activities of their departments as broad policy decisions are taken at the top and more specific decisions at lower levels.

System 4 is characterized by participative group management. Management give economic rewards and make full use of group participation and involvement in setting high performance goals, improving work methods, etc.; communication flows downwards, upwards and with peers and is accurate; subordinates and superiors are very close psychologically. Decision-making is widely done throughout the organization through group processes, and is integrated into the formal structure by regarding the organization chart as a series of overlapping groups with each group linked to the rest of the organization by means of persons (called 'linking pins') who are members of more than one group. System 4 management produces high productivity, greater involvement of individuals, and better labour–management relations.

In general, high-producing managers are those who have built the personnel in their units into effective groups, whose members have cooperative attitudes and a high level of job satisfaction through System 4 management. But there are exceptions. Technically competent, job-centred, tough management can achieve high productivity (particularly if backed up by tight systems of control techniques). But the members of units whose supervisors use these high-pressure methods are likely to have unfavourable attitudes towards their work and the management, and to have excessively high levels of waste and scrap. They also show higher labour turnover, and greater labour–management conflict as measured by work-stoppages, official grievances and the like.

Management, according to Likert, is always a relative process. To be effective and to communicate, leaders must always adapt their behaviour to take account of the *persons* whom they lead. There are no specific rules which will work well in all situations, but only general principles which must be interpreted to take account of the expectations, values and skills of those with whom the manager interacts. Sensitivity to these values and expectations is a crucial leadership skill, and organizations must create the atmosphere and conditions which encourage all managers to deal with the people they encounter in a manner fitting to their values and their expectations.

To assist in this task, management now has available a number of measures of relevant factors which have been developed by social scientists. Methods are available to obtain objective measurements of such variables as: the amount of member loyalty to an organization; the extent to which the goals of groups and individuals facilitate the achievement of the organization's goals; the level of motivation among members; the degree of confidence and trust between different hierarchical levels and between different sub-units; the efficiency and adequacy of the communication process; the extent to which superiors are correctly informed of the expectations, reactions, obstacles, problems and failures of subordinates – together with the assistance they find useful and the assurance they wish they could get.

These measures and others enable an organization to know at any time the state of the system of functioning human beings which underpins it (called the 'interaction-influence system'); whether it is improving or deteriorating and why, and what to do to bring about desired improvements. This objective information about the interaction-influence system enables problems of leadership and management to be depersonalized and the 'authority of facts' to come to the fore. A much wider range of human behaviour can now be measured and made objective, whereas previously impressions and judgements had to suffice.

Douglas McGregor examines the assumptions about human behaviour which underlie managerial action. The traditional conception of administration (as exemplified by the writings of Fayol, p. 85) is based upon the direction and control by management of the enterprise and its individual members. It implies certain basic assumptions about human motivation, which McGregor characterizes as 'Theory X'. These are:

1. The average human being has an inherent dislike of work and will avoid it if possible. Thus management needs to stress productivity, incentive schemes and 'a fair day's work': and to denounce 'restriction of output'.
2. Because of this human characteristic of dislike of work, most people must be coerced, controlled, directed, threatened with punishment to get them to put forth adequate effort toward the achievement of organizational objectives.
3. The average human being prefers to be directed, wishes to avoid responsibility, has relatively little ambition, wants security above all.

Theory X has persisted for a long time (although it is not usually stated as baldly as this). It has done so because it has undoubtedly provided an explanation for *some* human behaviour in organizations. There are, however, many readily observable facts and a growing body of research findings (such as those described by Likert) which cannot be explained on these assumptions. McGregor proposes an alternative 'Theory Y', with the underlying principle of 'integration' to replace direction and control. The assumptions about human motivation of Theory Y are:

1. The expenditure of physical and mental effort in work is as natural as play or rest. The ordinary person does not inherently dislike work: according to the conditions it may be a source of satisfaction or punishment.
2. External control is not the only means for obtaining effort. People will exercise self-direction and self-control in the service of objectives to which they are committed.
3. The most significant reward that can be offered in order to obtain commitment is the satisfaction of the individual's self-actualizing needs (compare Argyris, see p. 167). This can be a direct product of effort directed towards organizational objectives.
4. The average human being learns, under proper conditions, not only to accept but to seek responsibility.
5. Many more people are able to contribute creatively to the solution of organizational problems than do so.
6. At present the potentialities of the average person are not being fully used.

McGregor develops an analysis of how the acceptance of Theory Y as the basis for running organizations would work out. He is particularly concerned with effects on performance appraisals, salaries and promotions, participation and staff–line relationships. On this last topic he makes the important point that there will be tension and conflict between staff and line as long as the staff departments are used as a service to top management to *control* the line (which is required by Theory X). With Theory Y the role of the staff is regarded as that of providing professional help to *all levels* of management.

The essential concept which both Likert and McGregor are propounding is that modern organizations, to be effective, must regard themselves as interacting groups of people with '*supportive relationships*' to each other. In the ideal, all members will feel that the organization's objectives are of personal significance to them. They will regard their jobs, which contribute to the objectives, as meaningful, indispensable and difficult. Therefore, in order to do their jobs effectively, they need and obtain the support of their superiors. Superiors in turn regard their prime function as the giving of this support to make their subordinates effective.

In later work Likert and Likert extend the System 1 to 4 classification by identifying the 'System 4 Total Model Organization' (System 4T). This designation refers to organizations which have a number of characteristics in addition to those of System 4. These include: high levels of performance goals held by the leader and transmitted to subordinates; high levels of knowledge and skill of the leader with regard to technical issues, administration and problem-solving; the capacity of the leader to provide planning, resources, equipment, training and help to subordinates. System 4T is also characterized by an optimum structure in terms of differentiation and linkages, and stable group working relationships.

System 4T is currently the best method for dealing with conflict because of its approach of getting appropriate data related to *group* needs (thus removing person-to-person conflict) and engaging in group decision-making in order to resolve the differences in the best interests of the entire organization. If members of one or both of the two groups show an inability to use group decision-making techniques sufficiently well, then higher levels must provide further training in group processes. The interaction-influence system will develop a capacity for self-correction, since superiors recognize those groups which are not performing their linking-pin and problem-solving functions effectively and can arrange for coaching and training. Correction is possible because the failures are picked up not by after-the-fact data (e.g. falling production, rising costs, lower earnings) but through the interaction-influence system, in the early stages before poor performance and conflict arise.

Likert's argument is that the nearer to System 4T the organization approaches the more productivity and profits will improve and conflict be reduced. Likert also suggests a System 5 organization of the future in which the authority of hierarchy will completely disappear. The authority of individuals will derive only from their linking-pin roles and from the influence exerted by the overlapping groups of which they are members.

BIBLIOGRAPHY

LIKERT, R., *New Patterns of Management*, McGraw-Hill, 1961.

LIKERT, R., *The Human Organization: Its Management and Value*, McGraw-Hill, 1967.

MCGREGOR, D., *The Human Side of Enterprise*, McGraw-Hill, 1960.

MCGREGOR, D., *Leadership and Motivation*, M I T Press, 1966.

MCGREGOR, D., *The Professional Manager*, McGraw-Hill, 1967.

LIKERT, R., and LIKERT, J. G., *New Ways of Managing Conflict*, McGraw-Hill, 1976.

Robert R. Blake and Jane S. Mouton

Robert Blake and Jane Mouton are respectively Chairman and President of Scientific Methods, Inc., an organization which provides behavioural science consultancy services to industry. Both are psychologists, trained in American universities. Blake first designed and tested the 'Managerial Grid' during his subsequent employment in industry.

Blake and Mouton start from the assumption that a manager's job is to foster attitudes and behaviour which promote efficient performance, stimulate and use creativity, generate enthusiasm for experimentation and innovation, and learn from interaction with others. Such managerial competence can be taught and it can be learned. Their managerial grid provides a framework for understanding and applying effective management.

The grid sets the guidelines for an approach to management which has been widely applied. It has been successful in North America, in Europe, and in Asia; in production work, sales, and R & D, in trade unions, and in military, government, and welfare organizations. Its relevance appears to transcend cultural boundaries and forms of organization. Moreover, it has been applied from supervisory jobs to executive levels.

The managerial grid results from combining two fundamental ingredients of managerial behaviour. One is concern for production: the other is concern for people. 'Concern for' does not mean a dedication to specific targets, nor does it mean the results achieved in themselves. It means the general approach to management which governs the actions of managers, just *how* they concern themselves with production and with people.

Concern for production does not mean only physical factory products. The term 'production' can refer to the number of good research ideas, the number of accounts processed, the volume of sales, the quality of service given or of top policy decisions made, and so on. Concern for people similarly includes all of concern for friendships, for personal commitment to tasks, for someone's self-respect, for equitable payment, and so on.

Any manager's approach to management will show more or less of each of these two fundamental constituents. A manager may show a high degree of production concern together with low people concern, or the other way around, or may be middling on both. Indeed all of these are commonplace and it is also commonplace that none of these is satisfactory. Placing the two fundamentals as the axes of a graph enables a grid to be drawn which reveals very simply not only many typical combinations seen in the behaviour of managers every day, but also the desirable combination of 'concern for', as follows:

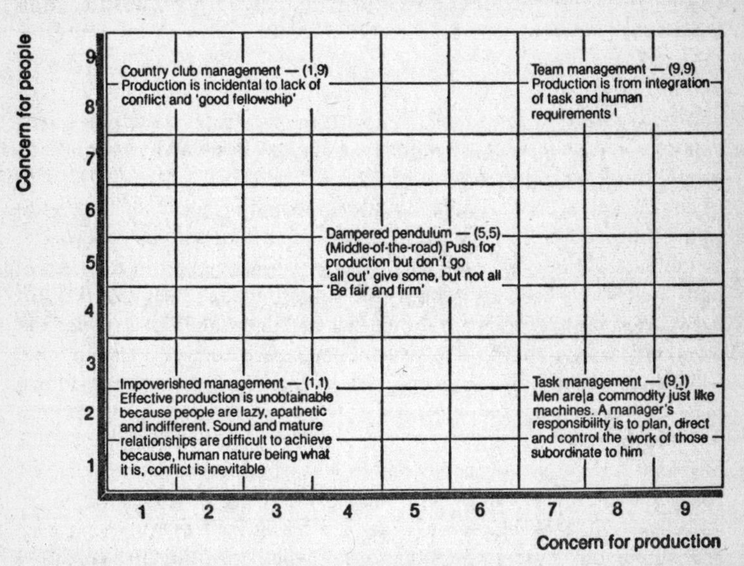

The Managerial Grid (from Blake and Mouton, 'The managerial grid', *Advanced Management Office Executive*, 1962, vol. 1, no. 9)

Different positions on the grid represent different typical patterns of behaviour. The grid suggests that change could be towards *both* high concern for production (scores 9) and high concern for people (also scores 9) simultaneously, that is to a 9,9 managerial style of 'team management'.

The grid indicates that all degrees of concern for production and concern for people are possible; but for simplicity five styles of management are picked out for illustration.

9,1 management, or 'task management', focuses overwhelmingly on production. A 9,1 manager is an exacting taskmaster who expects schedules to be met and people to do what they are told, no more and no less. Anything that goes wrong will be viewed as due to someone's mistake, and that someone must be found and that blame squarely placed. Supervisors make decisions. Subordinates carry them out. The manager should run the show, and disagreement is likely to be viewed as the next thing to insubordination. 9,1 management can achieve high production, at least in the short run, but it has a number of deficiencies. Any creative energies of subordinates go into how to defeat the system rather than how to improve it. Disagreements are ruled out and suppressed rather than settled. Subordinates do what is required, but no more, and seem 'obviously' indifferent and apathetic. Win–lose thinking is eventually reflected in the development of trade unions and struggles between unions and managements. 9,1 management is prevalent in a competitive industrial society such as the USA because inadequate education leaves many people unable to use more than limited skills and compelled to endure this kind of supervision.

The 1,9 managerial style, or 'country club management' as it has been called, emphasizes solely concern for people. It does not push people for production because 'you can lead a horse to water, but you can't make him drink'. People are encouraged and supported, and their mistakes are overlooked because they are doing the best they can. The key word is togetherness and informal conversation, coffee together, and a joke helps things along. The informal rule is 'no work discussions during breaks'. But country club management also has deficiencies. People try to avoid direct disagreements or criticisms of one another and production problems are glossed over. No one should be upset even if work is not going quite as it should. New ideas which might cause trouble or objectives which would cause strain are let slide. The 1,9 style easily grows up in quasi-monopoly situations or when operating on a cost-plus basis, and its ultimate end may be the complete closing of a non-competitive unit.

Little concern for either production or people results in 'impoverished management', the 1,1 style. It is difficult to imagine a whole organization surviving for long with this kind of management, but it is frequent enough in individual managers and supervisors. 1,1 management is characterized by the avoidance of responsibility or personal commitment, and by leaving people to work as they think fit. These leaders do just enough so that if anything goes wrong they can say 'I told them what to do – it's not my fault.' They minimize contacts with everyone, and are non-committal on any problems which come to them. The 1,1 approach typically reveals the frustrations of someone who has been passed over for promotion, shunted sideways, or has been for years in a routine job (as Argyris, p. 167, also suggests).

Managers frequently alternate between the 1,9 'country club' style and the 9,1 'task management' style. They tighten up to increase output,

9,1 style, but when human relationships begin to suffer the pendulum swings right across to 1,9 again. The middle of the managerial grid shows the 5,5 'dampened pendulum' style, typified by marginal shifts around the happy medium. This middle-of-the-road style pushes enough to get acceptable production but yields enough to maintain acceptable morale. To aim fully for both is too idealistic. Such managers aim at a moderate carrot-and-stick standard, fair but firm, and have confidence in their subordinates' ability to meet targets. 5,5 management thus gives rise to 'splitting the difference' on problems, to attempting balanced solutions rather than appropriate ones.

Unlike 5,5 management, and all the other styles, 9,9 'team management' shows high concern for production and high concern for people, and does not accept that these concerns are incompatible. The team manager seeks to integrate people around production. Morale is task-related. Unlike 5,5 the 9,9 style tries to discover the best and most effective solutions, and aims at the highest attainable production to which all involved contribute and find their own sense of accomplishment. People satisfy their own needs through the job and working with others, not through incidental sociability in the 'country club' style. The 9,9 manager assumes that employees who know what the stakes are for them and others in what they are doing will not need boss direction and control (as Likert, p. 156). The manager's responsibility is to see to it that work is planned and organized by those with a stake in it, not necessarily to do that task personally. Objectives should be clear to all; and, though demanding, should be realistic. It is accepted that conflict will occur, but problems are confronted directly and openly and not as personal disputes. This encourages creativity. Sustained improvement of the form of organization and development of those in it are both aims and likely outcomes of a 9,9 style.

Blake and Mouton reject most strongly a contingency approach to leadership and decision-making (see Fiedler, p. 181, and Vróom, p. 133). Contingency theorists argue that particular leadership styles are appropriate to particular situations. This is to say that there are certain circumstances where a 9,1 or a 1,9 style would be the most appropriate. Blake and Mouton dispute this very static approach for it does not appear to consider the adverse longer-term effects of, for example, a 9,1 style in the negative consequences for the leader's health and career, and the lack of growth in stunting of subordinates.

The 9,9 leadership style is always the best since it builds on long-term development and trust. A leader whose subordinates expect or want 9,1 or 1,9 leadership should train them so that they can understand and respond to 9,9. In this way their own development will be improved. The 9,9 approach should be adopted with versatility but the principles should be firmly retained.

In *Executive Achievement*, Blake and Mouton present eight case studies of top executives and use the Grid framework to analyse the limitations in leadership shown. Many of the habits which limit top management effectiveness have come about over the years in an unsystematic, even unthinking, way. Leaders can be encouraged to think more about how to behave effectively, and to gain personal insights on ways of changing. They are then prepared to change towards 9,9 leadership because the 'bottom line pay off' is so considerable.

For maximum effectiveness the whole culture of the organization must be changed to a 9,9 orientation, using a phased programme of organizational development. In Phase 1 the Managerial Grid is studied as a framework for understanding organizational behaviour through off-site training. Phase 2 focuses on the on-site training in problem-solving methods of actual functioning teams as a whole. The same kind of application is made in Phase 3 but to inter-group work between units of the company where cooperation and coordination are necessary. Phase 4 is concerned with setting group goals for the optimum performance of the total organization. In Phase 5 the resulting changes are implemented, and Phase 6 measures these changes in order to consolidate them and set new goals for the future. Where evaluation of this programme has been carried out the evidence points to more successful organizations and to greater career accomplishments by individual managers, as its results.

BIBLIOGRAPHY

BLAKE, R. R., and MOUTON, J. S., *The Versatile Manager: a Grid Profile*, Irwin-Dorsey, 1981.

BLAKE, R. R., and MOUTON, J. S., *The Managerial Grid III*, Gulf Publishing, 1985.

BLAKE, R. R., and MOUTON J. S., *Executive Achievement: Making it at The Top*, McGraw-Hill, 1986.

Chris Argyris

After taking his first degrees in psychology, Chris Argyris was for many years Professor of Industrial Administration at Yale University. Since 1971 he has been James Bryant Conant Professor of Education and Organizational Behaviour at Harvard University. He has consistently studied how the personal development of the individual is affected by the kind of situation in which that individual works. Argyris sees each person as having a potential which needs to be fully realized. Such self-actualization brings not only personal benefits but also benefits to the individual's working group and employing organization. Unfortunately, business and other institutions are usually run in a way which prevents any such benefits.

There are three sides to this problem: the development of the individual towards psychological maturity, the nature of the organization, and the degree of interpersonal competence shown by the supervisor and other members of the working group.

What adults do at work can be best understood by examining the extent to which they have matured from the infantile ways of babyhood. This progression from infancy towards maturity may be said to consist of seven developments:

1. From infant passivity towards adult activity.
2. From dependence towards relative independence.
3. From limited behaviours to many different behaviours.
4. From erratic, shallow, brief interests to more stable, deeper interests.
5. From short time perspective to longer time perspective.
6. From a subordinate social position to an equal or superordinate social position.
7. From lack of self-awareness to self-awareness and self-control.

Young children's interests and enjoyments shift from minute to minute, and are concerned only with the here and now. They cannot wait till later for the expected ice-cream. They are self-centred and unaware of how their demands affect others; but they accept a dependent position in which parents largely control what they do. Mature adulthood is achieved when individuals develop some ability to see themselves from the point of view of others, pursue interests consistently, foresee consequences even years ahead, and accept responsibilities for others.

With such development goes the possibility for the full and constructive release of psychological energy. Each individual has a set of needs and, if offered potential satisfaction and yet some challenge in the process, will put all such energies into meeting the challenge.

The trouble is that the typical approach to the management of organizations, and the lack of interpersonal competence in them, prevent people becoming mature in outlook and fail to arouse their full psychological energy. People too often remain short-sighted in their actions on the job, concerned with present advantage and unable to see future consequences; they shirk responsibility and are uninterested in opportunities; their approach to their work is apathetic. But the fault is not theirs individually.

In factories, in research organizations, in hospitals, among executives, among scientists, among technicians, on the shop floor, everywhere, Argyris's research suggests that interpersonal competence is low. That is, people find excuses for what they do, or don't stop to notice its effects on others; they only half hear what others try to tell them; they stick to their habitual ways and never try a new approach to someone else. The results are mutual suspicion and distrust, a tendency to avoid telling everything to the other person, and a reluctance in being honest about one's own feelings or those of the other person. In such a situation, people show a superficial 'pseudo-health' in which although there is no active dissatisfaction, each remains confined to minimum routine tasks in an indifferent manner, and refuses to look any further than these. True frankness of manner and commitment to the job are missing.

This atmosphere is common in formal 'rational' organizations. These are managed on the basis of reducing tasks to minimal specialized routines and establishing a chain of command by which people doing such tasks are instructed precisely what to do. As a result the specialists and departments follow their own ends irrespective of wider interests and even to each other's detriment.

In such organizations individuals cannot progress from infantile behaviour. In their limited routine tasks they look forward to the end of the day's work, but are unable to foresee the success or failure of the whole enterprise over a period of years. To their superiors their infuriating inability to see beyond the end of their noses and their own relatively trivial work difficulties are inexplicable. They have come to accept a passive and dependent position, without initiative.

Faced with this lack of response, even among lower managers or specialists, executives are liable to become yet more autocratic and directive. Their existing strong 'pyramidal values' are reinforced. The increased use of management controls deprives employees of any opportunity of participating in the important decisions which affect their working life, leading to feelings of psychological failure. It is not they themselves but control systems (such as work study and cost accounting) which define, inspect and evaluate the quality and quantity of their performance. And as subordinates tell less and less about what is happening, as everyone pays more attention to keeping up appearances ready for the next job-study investigation or tense budget allocation committee meeting, so less effort goes into the job itself.

These are some of the problems human beings have in relating to organizational life. Together with Donald A. Schon, Argyris has also examined some of the built-in contradictions that arise from the functioning of the organization itself which has the paradoxical requirement of both wanting to maintain stability and also be dynamic or changing. Thus typically organization members may be told: take initiatives *but* do not violate rules; think beyond the present *but* be rewarded and penalized on present performance only; think of the organization as a whole *but* do not cross into others' areas of responsibility; cooperate with others *but* compete with others when required.

The main problem is not that these contradictions exist, but that in the usual poor state of managerial interpersonal competence, they cannot be raised and discussed as issues. Although many managers may *talk* about the openness of communication and the participative approach of their organizations (what is called their 'espoused' theory), what they actually do may be very different. There are very strong defensive routines built into many managements' thinking, ensuring that they resist the openess which leads to interpersonal change.

Argyris and Schon have demonstrated that the basis of many managers' actions (called their 'theory-in-use') can be subsumed under four rules of behaviour, referred to as Model I: (i) design goals unilaterally and try to achieve them, (ii) maximize winning and minimize losing by controlling the task with as little dependence on others as possible, (iii) minimize generating or expressing negative feelings in public,keep your own thoughts and feelings a mystery, (iv) be rational and 'objective' and suppress the voicing of feelings by others, thus protecting yourself and them from facing important issues which often have an emotional content to them.

Managers who operate on Model I have a very unilateral view of their world in which they are striving to have complete control. Their aim is to defend themselves and impose on others. They thus generate mistrust and rigidity and are therefore confirmed in their Model I view that open discussion of issues is best avoided. The only learning that occurs is learning how to conform (called 'single-loop' learning) and the process becomes 'self-sealing'.

Argyris and Schon propose a Model II theory-in-use which does allow organizational learning. The norms here are: (i) take action on valid information and be open about obtaining it, (ii) take action after free and informed choice with all who are competent and relevant taking part, (iii) generate internal commitment to the choice with monitoring of implementation and preparedness to change. Managers who operate in a Model II world are not defensive and thus they can participate in 'double-loop' learning. They look for contributions from others who are competent; they are able to confront their own basic assumptions and take part in testing them in public, which allows of their changing.

The issue then becomes: if managers operating in a Model I 'mode' are by definition unaware of this fact since they are using defensive routines to resist change, how may they be helped to develop effective learning in Model II? Argyris proposes a training programme to bring out into the open these contradictions, in situations where managers' feelings of vunerability are reduced. Managers are helped by interpersonal consultants to confront the large gap which usually exists between what is said and done in a decision-making group and what is actually felt by the members. They can then analyse the defensive routines which they habitually use to stop openness and innovation and practise taking a Model II approach in their work.

BIBLIOGRAPHY

ARGYRIS, C., *Personality and Organization*, Harper & Row, 1957.
ARGYRIS, C., *Organization and Innovation*, Irwin, 1965.
ARGYRIS, C., and SCHON. D., *Organizational Learning: a Theory of Action Perspective*, Addison-Wesley, 1978.
ARGYRIS, C., *Strategy, Change and Defensive Routines*, Pitman, 1985.

Edgar H. Schein

Edgar H. Schein has been for many years Professor of Management at the Sloan School of Management of the Massachusetts Institute of Technology. A social psychologist by training, in his early years at MIT he was a junior colleague of Douglas McGregor (see p. 156) whose personality and work had much influence on him. Working in that tradition, Schein has been an influential researcher, consultant and writer on issues concerned with organizational behaviour, particularly individual motivation, career dynamics and organizational culture.

Schein's analysis of motivation begins, like McGregor's, with an examination of the underlying assumptions that managers make about the people they manage. He suggests three sets of assumptions, roughly in order of their historical appearance, and adds a fourth which he considers more appropriate.

1. The *Rational-economic Model* is the mental picture held by managers who consider workers to be primarily motivated by economic incentives as manipulated by the organization. The worker is essentially passive, lazy, unwilling to take responsibility and must therefore be controlled by the manager. This is the basis of Taylor's approach to management (see p. 90), which is expounded by McGregor (see p. 158) as Theory X. This approach led to the possibility of mass-production industry, but broke down when unions became powerful, and jobs became more complex requiring more of an employee than being just a 'pair of hands'.
2. The *Social Model* developed from awareness of the worker's needs for identity through relationships with others, particularly the working group. The group's norms and pressures have much more power over production than do formal incentive systems and management controls. The work of Mayo and the Hawthorne investigations (see p. 152) had an important impact in changing managerial ideas, as did the study by Trist and his colleagues of mining (see p. 186). The implications for managers are spelled out in Likert's work on the need for 'employee-centred' leadership and participative group management (see p. 156).
3. The *Self-actualizing Model* is a further development which underlines

that typically organizations remove the meaning of any work that employees do. The inherent need of workers to exercise their understanding, capacities and skills in an adult way is thus frustrated, and alienation and dissatisfaction ensue. The analysis of the clinical psychologist, Abraham Maslow, has been very influential here. He maintains that 'self-actualization' (the realization of one's distinctive psychological potential) is the highest form of human need, going beyond economic and social fulfilment. The implications of this approach are developed for managers in McGregor's Theory Y (see p. 159), Argyris's Model II (see p. 169) and Herzberg's Job Enrichment (see p. 176).

4. The *Complex Model*, developed by Schein, maintains that earlier theories are based on conceptions which are too simplified and generalized. Human needs fall into many categories and vary according to the person's stage of personal development and life situation. So motives will vary from one person to another, one situation to another, one time to another. Incentives can also vary in their impact: money, for example, usually satisfying basic economic needs can also serve to satisfy self-actualization needs for some. What motivates millionaires to go on to make their second or fifth million? Employees are also capable of learning new motives through organizational experiences, and can respond to different kinds of managerial strategies.

The most important implication for managers is that they need to be good diagnosticians. They should be flexible enough to vary their own behaviour in relation to the need to treat in an appropriate way particular subordinates in particular situations. They may require to use any of the economic, social or self-actualizing models. They may use 'scientific management' in the design of some jobs, but allow complete group autonomy for the workers to organize themselves in others. They would thus use a 'contingency approach' as exemplified by Lawrence and Lorsch (see p. 45), Vroom (see p. 133), and Fiedler (see p. 181), among others.

According to Schein the key factor which determines the motivation of individuals in organizations is the psychological contract. This is the unwritten set of expectations operating at all times between every member of an organization and those who represent the organization itself to that member. It includes economic components (pay, working hours, job security, etc.) but it will also include more implicit concerns such as being treated with dignity, obtaining some degree of work autonomy, having opportunities to learn and develop. Some of the strongest feelings leading to strikes and employee turnover have to do with violations of these implicit components, even though the public negotiations are about pay and conditions of work.

The organization, too, has implicit expectations: that employees will be loyal, will keep trade secrets, will do their best on behalf of the organization, etc. Whether individuals will work with commitment and enthusiasm is the result of a matching between the two components. On the one side, their own expectations of what the organization will provide to them and what they should provide in return; on the other, the organization's expectations of what it will give and get. The degree to which these correspond will determine the individual's motivation. The degree of matching is liable to change and the psychological contract is therefore continually being renegotiated, particularly during the progress of an individual's career.

The 'career development perspective' taken by Schein sees the continual matching process between the individual and the organization as the key to understanding both human resource planning for the organization and career planning for the individual. This matching is particularly important at certain key transitions in a career, such as initial entry into the organization, moving from technical to managerial work, changing from being 'on the way up' to 'levelling off' and so on.

A crucial element in the matching is the nature of the *career anchor* that the individual holds. This is the self-perceived set of talents, motives and attitudes, based on actual experiences, which is developed by each individual particularly in the early years of an organizational career. It provides a growing area of stability within the individual's attitudes which anchors the interpretation of career and life options. Typical career anchors found by Schein in a detailed longitudinal study of MIT management graduates include those of technical competence, managerial competence, security and autonomy. Career anchors affect considerably the way individuals see themselves, their jobs and their organizations. For example, one graduate using a technical competence anchor was still, in mid-career, only concerned with technical tasks. He refused to become involved in aspects of sales or general management even though he was now a director and part owner of the firm in which he worked. Another graduate, using managerial competence as an anchor, left one firm although his bosses were quite pleased with his performance. But he considered that he only actually worked two hours a day, and he was not satisfied with that.

The understanding of the dynamics of career development is important in enabling Human Resource Planning and Development to improve the matching processes between individual and organization needs so that early-, mid- and late-career crises can be dealt with more effectively.

A distinctive aspect of the way that an organization functions, which shapes its overall performance as well as the feelings which individuals have about it, is its culture. This is the pattern of basic assumptions developed by an organization as it learns to cope with problems of external adaptation and internal integration. These assumptions are taught to new members as the correct way to perceive, think and feel in order to be successful. They cover a wide range of issues: how to dress, how much to argue, how far to defer to the boss's authority, what to reward and what to punish, are some of them. Organizations develop very wide differences on these topics.

Leaders play a key role in maintaining and transmitting the culture. They do this by a number of powerful mechanisms. What they pay attention to, measure and control; how they react to a range of crises; who they recruit, promote, excommunicate; all these send important messages about the kind of organization they are running. The key to leadership is managing cultural change.

The considerable difficulties that almost inevitably beset the establishment of an effective organization after a merger of two companies underline the need to understand the nature of cultural differences and how cultural change can be consciously managed. The big danger is that the acquiring company will not only impose its own structures and procedures but also its own philosophy, value systems and managerial style on a situation for which it has no intuitive 'feel' Thus a large packaged foods manufacturer purchased a chain of successful fast-food restaurants. They imposed many of their manufacturing control procedures on the new subsidiary, which drove costs up and restaurant managers out. These were replaced by parent-company managers who did not really understand the technology and hence were unable to make effective use of the marketing techniques. Despite ten years of effort they could not run it profitably and had to sell it at a considerable loss.

Similar problems occur when organizations diversify into new product lines, new areas or new markets. Afterwards managers frequently say that cultural incompatabilities were at the root of the troubles, but somehow these factors rarely get taken into account at the time. One reason is that the culture of an organization is so pervasive that it is very difficult for members to identify its components in their own situation. They only recognize their own characteristics when they run up against problems due to differences in others. Schein presents a series of diagnostic procedures which would enable managers (usually with the help of an outside consultant) to uncover the cultural assumptions of their own organization and thus gain insight into its compatability with others.

BIBLIOGRAPHY

SCHEIN E. H., *Organizational Psychology*, 3rd edn, Prentice-Hall, 1980.

SCHEIN, E. H., *Career Dynamics: Matching Individual and Organizational Needs*, Addison-Wesley, 1978.

SCHEIN, E. H., *Organizational Culture and Leadership*, Jossey-Bass, 1985.

Frederick Herzberg

Frederick Herzberg is Distinguished Professor of Management in the University of Utah. After training as a psychologist he studied Industrial Mental Health. For many years he has, with colleagues and students, been conducting a programme of research and application on human motivation in the work situation and its effects on the individual's job satisfaction and mental health. He questions whether current methods of organizing work in business and industry are appropriate for people's total needs and happiness.

Herzberg and his colleagues conducted a survey of two hundred engineers and accountants representing a cross-section of Pittsburg industry. They were asked to remember times when they felt exceptionally good about their jobs. The investigators probed for the reasons why they felt as they did, asking for a description of the sequence of events which gave that feeling. The questions were then repeated for sequences of events which made them feel exceptionally bad about their jobs. The responses were then classified by topic in order to determine what type of events led to job satisfaction and job dissatisfaction.

The major finding of the study was that the events that led to satisfaction were of quite a different kind from those that led to dissatisfaction. Five factors stood out as strong determinants of job satisfaction: achievement, recognition, the attraction of the work itself, responsibility, and advancement. Lack of these five factors, though, was mentioned very infrequently in regard to job *dis*satisfaction. When the reasons for the dissatisfaction were analysed they were found to be concerned with a different range of factors: company policy and administration, supervision, salary, interpersonal relations and working conditions. Since such distinctly separate factors were found to be associated with job satisfaction and job dissatisfaction, Herzberg concludes that these two feelings are not the opposites to one another, rather they are concerned with two different ranges of human needs.

The set of factors associated with job dissatisfaction are those stemming from the individual's overriding need to avoid physical and social deprivation. Using a biblical analogy, Herzberg relates these to the 'Adam' conception of the nature of mankind. When Adam was expelled from the Garden of Eden he was immediately faced with the task of satisfying the needs which stem from his animal nature: the needs for food, warmth, avoidance of pain, safety, security, belongingness, etc. Ever since then people have had to concern themselves with the satisfaction of these needs together with those which, as a result of social conditioning, have been added to them. Thus, for example, we have learned that in certain economies the satisfaction of these needs makes it necessary to earn money which has therefore become a specific motivating drive.

In contrast, the factors associated with job satisfaction are those stemming from people's need to realize their human potential for perfection. In biblical terms this is the 'Abraham' conception of the nature of mankind. Abraham was created in the image of God. He was capable of great accomplishments, of development, of growth, of transcending his environmental limitations, of self-realization. People have these aspects to their natures too, they are indeed the characteristically human ones. They have needs to understand, to achieve, and through achievement to experience psychological growth, and these needs are very powerful motivating drives.

Both the Adam and Abraham natures of mankind look for satisfaction in work, but they do so in different ranges of factors. The Adam nature seeks the avoidance of dissatisfaction and is basically concerned with the job environment. It requires effective company policies, working conditions, security, pay, etc. and is affected by inadequacies in these. Since they are extrinsic to the job itself, Herzberg refers to them as 'job hygiene' or 'maintenance' factors. Just as lack of hygiene will cause disease, but the presence of hygienic conditions will not, of themselves, produce health, so lack of adequate 'job hygiene' will cause dissatisfaction, but their presence will not of themselves cause satisfaction. Satisfaction in work is provided through the Abraham nature which is concerned with the job content of the work itself, with achievement, recognition, responsibility, advancement, etc. These are the motivator or growth factors and their presence will cause satisfaction. Their absence will not cause dissatisfaction (if the job hygiene factors are adequate) but will lead to an absence of positive satisfactions. It is thus basic to Herzberg's approach that job satisfaction and job dissatisfaction are not opposites, since they are concerned with different factors in work serving different aspects of human nature. The opposite of job satisfaction, therefore, is not job dissatisfaction but simply no job satisfaction. The opposite of job dissatisfaction, similarly, is lack of job dissatisfaction.

The finding of the original study – that the factors associated with job satisfaction were basically different in kind from those associated with job dissatisfaction – has been repeated in several subsequent studies. Collating the information based on twelve different investigations, involving over one thousand six hundred employees in a variety of jobs in business and other organizations and in a number of countries, Herzberg presents results to show that the overwhelming majority of the factors contributing to job satisfaction (81 per cent) were the motivators concerned with growth and development. A large majority of the factors contributing to job dissatisfaction (69 per cent) involved hygiene or environmental maintenance.

How, then, may this 'motivation-hygiene' approach be used to increase the motivation and job satisfaction of employees? First, it is clear that this cannot be done through the job hygiene factors. Certainly, these can and should be improved as they will reduce job dissatisfaction, but adequate company policies, working conditions, pay and supervision, are increasingly thought of as a right to be expected, not as an incentive to greater achievement and satisfaction. For this, the rewarding nature of the work itself, recognition, responsibility, opportunities for achievement and advancement are necessary. Herzberg recognizes that these are phrases that may be used nowadays in relation to jobs, but they are often used in a superficial way, or as inspirational talk without much effective action. He therefore advocates an industrial engineering approach, based on the design of jobs, but from the opposite point of view from that of Taylor (see p. 90). Instead of rationalizing and simplifying the work to increase efficiency, the motivation-hygiene theory suggests that jobs be enriched to include the motivating factors in order to bring about an effective utilization of people and to increase job satisfaction.

The principles of *job enrichment* require that the job be developed to include new aspects which provide the opportunity for the employee's psychological growth. It is important that the new aspects are capable of allowing this. Merely to add one undemanding job to another (as is often the case with job enlargement) or to switch from one undemanding job to another (as in job rotation) is not adequate. These are merely horizontal job loading. In contrast, job enrichment calls for vertical job loading, where opportunities for achievement, responsibility, recognition, growth and learning are designed into the job. The approach would be to look for ways of removing some controls while retaining or increasing individuals' accountability for their own work; giving a person a complete natural unit of work; granting additional authority to an employee in the job; increasing job freedom; making reports directly available to the worker personally rather than to the supervisor; introducing new and more difficult tasks not previously undertaken, etc.

A number of experiments have been reported by Herzberg and his colleagues where these changes have been introduced with considerable effect. For example, in a study of the job of 'stockholder correspondent' of a large corporation the following suggestions were considered but rejected as involving merely horizontal job loading: firm fixed quotas could be set for letters to be answered each day, the employees could type the letters themselves as well as composing them, all difficult inquiries could be channelled to a few workers so that the rest could achieve high rates of output, the workers could be rotated through units handling different inquiries and then sent back to their own units. Instead, changes leading to the enrichment of jobs were introduced such as: correspondents were made directly responsible for the quality and accuracy of letters which were sent out directly over their names (previously a verifier had checked all letters, the supervisor had rechecked and signed them and was responsible for their quality and accuracy), subject-matter experts were appointed within each unit for other members to consult (previously the supervisor had dealt with all difficult and specialized questions), verification of experienced workers' letters was dropped from 100 per cent to 10 per cent and correspondents were encouraged to answer letters in a more personalized way instead of relying upon standard forms. In these ways, the jobs were enriched with resulting increases in both performance and job satisfaction.

In other studies, laboratory technicians ('experimental officers') were encouraged to write personal project reports in addition to those of the supervising scientists and were authorized to requisition materials and equipment direct; sales representatives were made wholly responsible for determining the calling frequencies on their customers and were given a discretionary range of about 10 per cent on the prices of most products; factory supervisors were authorized to modify schedules, to hire labour against agreed manning targets, to appoint their deputies, and so on. In each case, the results in both performance and satisfaction were considerable.

The more subordinates' jobs become enriched, the more superfluous does 'on the job' supervision in the old sense become. But this does not downgrade the supervisors' job; in the companies studied they found themselves free to develop more important aspects of their jobs with a greater managerial component than they had had time to before. It soon becomes clear that supervising people who have authority of their own is a more demanding, rewarding and enjoyable task than checking on every move of circumscribed automatons. For management the challenge is task organization to call out the motivators, and task support to provide adequate hygiene through company policy, technical supervision, working conditions, etc., thus satisfying both the Adam and the Abraham natures of mankind in work.

BIBLIOGRAPHY

HERZBERG, F., *Work and the Nature of Man*, World Publishing Co., 1966.

HERZBERG, F., 'One more time: How do you motivate employees?' *Harvard Business Review* 46 (1968), 53–62.

HERZBERG, F., *Managerial Choice: To Be Efficient and To Be Human*, Dow Jones-Irwin, 1976.

HERZBERG, F., MAUSNER, B., and SNYDERMAN, B., *The Motivation to Work*, Wiley, 1959.

PAUL, W. J., JR, ROBERTSON, K. B., and HERZBERG, F., 'Job enrichment pays off', *Harvard Business Review* 47 (1969), 61–78.

Fred E. Fiedler

Fred Fiedler is Professor of Psychology and Management at the University of Washington and Director of the Organizational Research Group. For over two decades he has been concerned with a research and consulting programme into the nature of effective leadership which has been carried out in a large range of organizations including business concerns, governmental agencies (both civil and military) and voluntary organizations.

Fiedler's studies of leadership have concentrated on work groups rather than the organization of which the group is a part. He assumes that those who are appointed leaders will have the requisite technical qualifications for the job (e.g. the Director of Product Development in a manufacturing firm will be an engineer, only qualified social workers will become Heads of Social Work Departments). He therefore asks what is it about the leadership behaviour *per se* which leads to effective group working. Effectiveness is defined, in a very 'hard-nosed' way, as how well the group performs the primary task for which it exists, e.g. output levels for managers of manufacturing departments, students' standardized achievement-test grades for school principals.

Focusing on the behaviour of the leader, Fiedler identifies two main leadership styles. *Relationship-motivated leaders* get their major satisfaction from good personal relationships with others. Their self-esteem depends very much on how others regard them, and they are sensitive to, and very concerned about, what their group members feel. They encourage subordinates to participate and to offer ideas.

Task-motivated leaders, on the other hand, are strongly concerned to complete successfully any task they have undertaken. They run a 'tight ship' with clear orders and standardized procedures for subordinates, and in their turn feel most comfortable working from their superiors' clear guidelines and operating procedures. If these are missing they will try to create them.

Fiedler has developed a very distinctive measure to classify these two styles or motivation patterns. The questionnaire measure asks leaders to review all the people with whom they have ever worked and think of the one with whom they could work least well. They are then asked to rate this *Least Preferred Co-worker* (LPC) on a number of characteristics.

Relationship-motivated leaders are those who will score these characteristics highly in spite of their difficulties with their LPC. Thus they may rate their choice as untrustworthy and inconsiderate but will admit that the LPC was cheerful, warm and relaxed. Since relationships are important to them, this type of leader will make these detailed discriminations to treat their choice fairly.

Task-motivated leaders rate people in terms of their ability to contribute to the successful achievement of the group's task, so they will rate their LPC very low indeed – and it will be a blanket poor evaluation. Thus the LPC would be not only unpleasant and disloyal, but also tense, boring, insincere and quarrelsome as well!

In all his work Fiedler emphasizes very strongly that *both* these leadership styles can be effective in appropriate situations. Thus he takes a contingency approach to leadership and rejects the conception that there is a best style that is appropriate for all situations (cf. Likert and McGregor, p. 156; Blake and Mouton, p. 162). What is effective leadership will be contingent on the nature of the tasks which leaders face and the situations in which they operate.

The underlying concept which is used to characterize the situation of the leader is that of favourableness, in terms of the ability to exercise power and influence. The more power the leader has, the greater the influence and control, the less the dependence on the goodwill of others, then the easier will be the leadership task. Three dimensions are used to analyse the situation:

1. *Leader–member relations:* Leaders who have good relationships with their group members, who are liked and respected, will have more influence than those with poor relationships. Fiedler claims that this is the most important single dimension.
2. *Task structure:* Tasks or assignments which are spelled out with specific guidelines, or even programmed, give the leader more influence than tasks which are vague, nebulous and unstructured.
3. *Leader's position power:* Leaders who are able to reward and punish subordinates (through disciplining, setting pay, hiring and firing, etc.) have more power and are thus in a more controlling and favourable position than those who cannot.

Ordering leadership situations as being either high or low on each of these three dimensions generates an eight cell classification which is listed along the horizontal axis of the figure opposite. This is a scale of favourableness for the leader.

An example of a leader in 'Octant 1', the most favourable situation, might be a construction superintendent building a bridge from a set of blueprints, who has personally hired the work crews and has their full

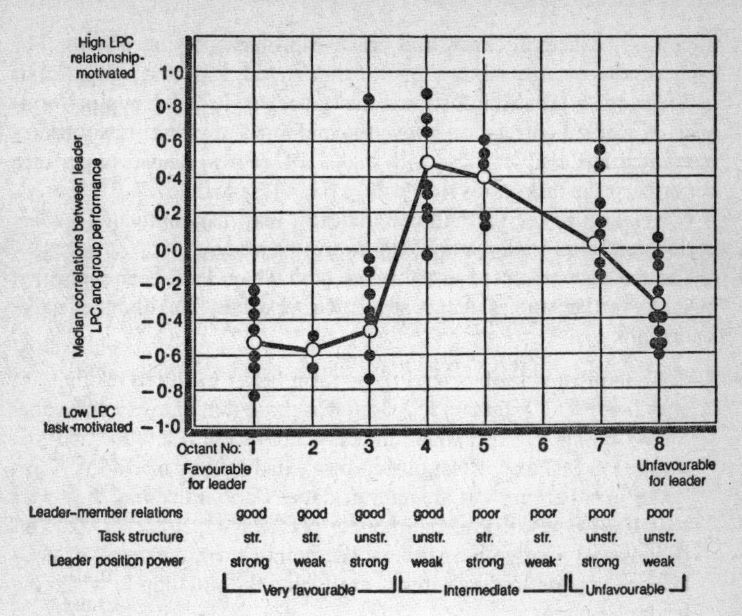

from Fiedler (1972)

support. The *technical* task may be difficult but, because it is structured and spelled out and the leader has good relations and strong power, the *leadership* task is the easiest and the leader has a great deal of control.

In contrast, an example of an 'Octant 8' situation might be that of a parent who has taken on the task of chairing a committee of the Parent–Teachers Association to organize an outing 'so that everybody can have a good time'. Here the *technical* task is much easier than building a bridge but the *leadership* task is much more difficult – since the task is very unstructured (how do you determine whether everybody has had a good time?), the parent has weak position power (not being able to order the committee to carry out instructions) and many may resent the appointment anyway (poor leader–member relations).

In between these two extreme examples fall many leadership situations (classified as 'Octants 2 to 7') where some aspects of the situation are favourable to the leader but others are not.

The critical question then becomes: what kind of leadership (relationship-motivated or task-motivated) does each of these octants call for? The figure presents the results of Fiedler's wide-ranging studies, based on many hundreds of work groups and covering the whole range of octants. The groups included bomber and tank crews, boards of directors, basketball teams and creative problem-solving groups. For each of the octants (shown on the horizontal axis) the vertical axis indicates the relationship between the leader's style and group performance. A median correlation above the mid-line shows that relationship-motivated leaders (i.e. those with high LPC scores) tended to perform better than the task-motivated leaders (i.e. those with low LPC scores). A correlation below the mid-line indicates that task-motivated leaders performed better than relationship-motivated leaders.

The findings presented in the figure (and which have been replicated by many further studies) demonstrate two important facts about effective leadership:

1. Task-motivated leaders tend to perform better in situations that are very favourable (Octants 1, 2, 3) and in those that are very unfavourable (Octants 7, 8) i.e. where the correlations fall below the mid-line on the vertical axis. Relationship-motivated leaders tend to perform better in situations that are intermediate in favourableness. It is clear that both types of leadership styles perform well under some conditions and poorly under others. We cannot therefore speak of poor leaders or good leaders without examining the situation in which the leader functions.
2. The performance of the leader depends as much on situational favourableness as it does on the style of the person in the leadership position. The crucial factor is that the style of the leader and the work group situation should be matched. This *leader match* and its appropriate benefits can be obtained either by trying to change the leader's style or by trying to change the leadership situation.

Fiedler has consistently maintained that the first of the change options to achieve leader match (changing the leader's style) is unrealistic and that leadership training which attempts to do this (e.g. to increase openness or employee-centredness) has not been effective because the leadership-style motivational pattern is too stable a characteristic of the individual (see Vroom, p. 133, for an opposing view). From Fiedler's point of view, what appropriate training does – together with experience – is to give the leader more technical knowledge and administrative know-how. This allows more influence and control and thus the situation becomes more favourable. But the contingency approach indicates that in many of the octants a more favourable situation (e.g. moving from Octant 8 to Octant 4 by improving leader–member relations) requires a different leadership style. Hence while training and experience will improve the performance of one type of leader where the new octant situation would now be matched to the style, it will *decrease* the performance of the other style type which has now lost its matching. Training must therefore be undertaken with a knowledge of leadership style in relation to leaders' situations, otherwise on average it is bound to have no effect.

Changing the situations in which leaders operate to those which call for their particular styles is a more appropriate way of achieving the leader match. Thus we might increase the favourableness of a task-motivated leader's situation to one which made a better match by giving more explicit instructions to work to, and more authority to achieve the tasks (Octant 4 to Octant 1). *Decreasing* the favourableness of the situation in order to improve the leader's performance by a better match is not as unusual as it first might appear. Managers are frequently transferred to more 'challenging' jobs because they have become bored or stale. 'Challenging' could well mean that there are awkward people to work with and the authority is much diminished. But the move of a relationship-motivated leader from Octant 1 to Octant 6 would improve the match and the leader's subsequent performance.

In later work, the importance of a leader's cognitive ability as an additional factor in determining the group's effectiveness is explored. The task-motivated style works when linked to high leader intelligence and a supportive environment. To be successful, leaders who are less intelligent in relation to their groups have to be relationship-motivated, in order to draw on the resources of their followers. These are key considerations in determining where a leader should be placed. In general successful organizations are those which give all leaders a good evaluation of their own characteristics and their group's performance, and which make them aware of the situations in which they perform best. Good leaders will create situations in which their cognitive capacity and leadership style are most likely to succeed.

BIBLIOGRAPHY

FIEDLER, F. E., *A Theory of Leadership Effectiveness*, McGraw-Hill, 1967.

FIEDLER, F. E., CHEMERS, M. M., and MAHAR, L., *Improving Leadership Effectiveness: the Leader Match Concept* (rev. edn), Wiley, 1977.

FIEDLER, F. E.., 'Situational Control and a Dynamic Theory of Leadership' from B. King *et al* (eds.) *Managerial Control and Organizational Democracy*, Wiley, 1978; reprinted in D. S. Pugh (ed.) *Organizational Theory*, Penguin, 1990.

FIEDLER, F. E., and GARCIA, J. E., *New Approaches to Effective Leadership: Cognitive Resources and Organizational Performance*, Wiley, 1987

Eric Trist and the work of the Tavistock Institute

Eric Trist is a social psychologist who for over twenty years was the senior member of the Tavistock Institute of Human Relations, London. During that time he conducted, with a number of colleagues (including F. E. Emery and the late A. K. Rice), a programme of research and consultancy investigations into the structure and functioning of organizations from a 'systems' point of view. He is currently affiliated with the Wharton School of the University of Pennsylvania where he is Emeritus Professor and Chairman of the Management and Behavioral Science Research Center, and with York University, Ontario, where he is Professor of Environmental Studies.

In collaboration with K. W. Bamforth (an ex-miner) Trist studied the effects of mechanization in British coal mining. With the advent of coal-cutters and mechanical conveyors, the degree of technical complexity of coal getting was raised to a higher level. Mechanization made possible the working of a single long face in place of a series of short faces, but this technological change had a number of social and psychological consequences for the work organization and the worker's place in it, to which little thought was given before the change was introduced. The pattern of organization in short face working was based on a small artisan group of a skilled man and his mate, assisted by one or more labourers. The basic pattern around which the work relationships in the longwall method were organized is the coal face group of forty to fifty men, their shot-firer and 'deputies' (i.e. supervisors). Thus the basic unit in mining took on the characteristics in size and structure of a small factory department, and in doing so disrupted the traditional high degree of job autonomy and close work relationships with a number of deleterious effects.

The mass production character of the longwall method necessitates a large-scale mobile layout advancing along the seam, basic task specialization according to shift, and very specific job roles with different methods of payment within each shift. In these circumstances there are considerable problems of maintaining effective communications and good working relations between forty men spatially spread over two hundred yards in a tunnel, and temporally spread over twenty-four hours in three successive shifts. From the production engineering point of view it is possible to write an equation that 200 tons equals 40 men over 200 yards over 24 hours, but the psychological and social problems raised are of a new order when the work organization transcends the limits of the traditional, small face-to-face group undertaking the complete task itself. The social integration of the previous small groups having been disrupted by the new technology, and little attempt made to achieve any new integration, many symptoms of social stress occur. Informal cliques which develop to help each other out can only occur over small parts of the face, inevitably leaving some isolated; individuals react defensively using petty deceptions with regard to timekeeping and reporting of work; they compete for allocation to the best workplaces; there is mutual scapegoating across shifts, each blaming the other for inadequacies (since in the new system with its decreased autonomy, no one individual can normally be pinpointed with the blame, scapegoating of the absent shift becomes self-perpetuating and resolves nothing). Absenteeism becomes a way of the miner compensating himself for the difficulties of the job.

This study of the effects of technological change led Trist to develop the concept of the working group as being neither a technical system nor a social system, but as an interdependent socio-technical system. The technological demands place limits on the type of work organization possible, but the work organization has social and psychological properties of its own that are independent of the technology. From this point of view it makes as little sense to regard social relationships as being determined by the technology as it does to regard the manner in which a job is performed as being determined by the social-psychological characteristics of the workers. The social and technical requirements are mutually interactive and they must also have economic validity, which is a third interdependent aspect. The attainment of optimum conditions for any one of these aspects does not necessarily result in optimum conditions for the system as a whole, since interference will occur if the others are inadequate. The aim should be joint optimization.

In further studies of mining, Trist found that it was possible, within the same technological and economic constraints, to operate different systems of work organization with different social and psychological effects, thus underlining the considerable degree of organizational choice which is available to management to enable them to take account of the social and psychological aspects. A third form of operation known as the 'composite longwall method' was developed which enabled mining to benefit from the new technology while at the same time allowing some of the characteristics of the shortwall method to be continued. In the composite system, groups of men are responsible for the whole task, allocate themselves to shifts and to jobs within the shift, and are paid on a group bonus. Thus the problems of over-specialized work roles, segregation of tasks across shifts with consequent scapegoating and lack of group cohesion were overcome. For example, it became common for a sub-group that had finished its scheduled work for a shift before time, to carry on with the next activity in the sequence in order to help those men on the subsequent shift who were members of their group. The composite longwall method was quite comparable in technological terms with the conventional longwall method, but it led to greater productivity, lower cost, considerably less absenteeism and accidents, and greater work satisfaction, since it was a socio-technical system which was better geared to the workers' social and psychological needs for job autonomy and close working relationships.

This socio-technical system approach was also applied to supervisory roles by Rice in studies of an Indian textile firm. He found that it was not enough to allocate to the supervisor a list of responsibilities (see Fayol, p. 85) and perhaps insist upon a particular style of handling workers (see Likert, p. 156). The supervisor's problems arise from a need to control and coordinate a system of worker–task relationships, and in particular to manage the 'boundary conditions', that is, those activities of this system which relate it to the larger system of which it is a part. In order to do this effectively, it is necessary to have an easily identifiable arrangement of tasks so that it is possible to maximize the autonomous responsibility of the group itself for its own internal control, thus freeing the supervisor for the key task of boundary management.

In an automatic weaving shed for example, in which the occupational roles had remained unchanged since hand weaving, the activities of the shed were broken down into component tasks, with the number of workers required determined by work studies of the separate tasks. Those in different occupational tasks worked on different numbers of looms; weavers operated 24 or 32, battery fillers charged the batteries of 48, smash hands served 75, jobbers 112, the bobbin carrier 224, etc. This resulted in the shift manager having to interact about the job regularly with all the remaining 28 workers on the shift, jobbers having to interact with 14, smash hands with 9, a weaver with 7, etc., all on the basis of individual interactions aggregated together only at the level of the whole shift, with no stable internal group structure. Rice carried through a reorganization to create 4 groups of 6 workers each with a group leader, each with an identifiable group task and a new set of interdependent work roles to carry it out. The boundaries of these groups were more easily delineated, and thus the work leader's task in their management facilitated. As a result there was a considerable and sustained improvement in efficiency and decrease in damage.

These studies and others of the Tavistock Institute have led Emery and Trist to conceptualize the enterprise as an 'open socio-technical system'. 'Open' because it is a system concerned with obtaining inputs from its environment and exporting outputs to its environment, as well as operating the conversion process in between. They regard the organization not in terms of a closed physical system which can obtain a stable resolution of forces in static equilibrium, but in the light of the biological concept of an open system (due to von Bertalanffy) in which the equilibrium obtained by the organism or the organization is essentially dynamic having a continual interchange across the boundaries with its environment. Indeed, they would regard the primary task of the management of the enterprise as a whole as that of relating the total system to its environment through the regulation of the boundary interchanges, rather than that of internal regulation. A management which takes its environment as given and concentrates on organizing internally in the most efficient way is pursuing a dangerous course. This does not mean that top management should not be involved in internal problems, but that such involvement must be oriented to the environmental opportunities and demands.

The problem is that environments are changing at an increasing rate and towards increasing complexity. Factors in the environment, over which the organization has no control or even no knowledge, may interact to cause significant changes. Emery and Trist have classified environments according to their degree of complexity from that of a placid, randomized environment (corresponding to the economist's perfect competition) to that of a 'turbulent field' in which significant variances arise not only from competitive organizations involved but also from the field (e.g. market) itself.

They present a case history of an organization which failed to appreciate that its environment was changing from a relatively placid to a relatively turbulent one. This company in the British food canning industry had, for a long period, held 65 per cent of the market for its main product – a tinned vegetable. On this basis the company invested in a new automatic factory, and in doing so incorporated an inbuilt rigidity – the necessity for long runs. But even while the factory was being built, several changes in the environment were taking place over which the organization had no control. The development of frozen foods, and the increasing affluence which enabled more people to afford these, presented consumers with an alternative. Greater direct competition came from the existence of surplus crops which American frozen food manufacturers sold off very cheaply due to their inappropriateness for freezing, their use by a number of small British *fruit* canning firms with surplus capacity due to the seasonal nature of imported fruit, and the development of supermarkets and chain stores with a wish to sell more goods under their house names. As the small canners provided an extremely cheap article (having no marketing costs and a cheaper raw material) they were able within three years to capture over 50 per cent of a shrinking market through supermarket own label channels. This is a clear example of the way in which factors in the environment interact directly to produce a considerable turbulence in the field of the organization's operations, which, in the case of the vegetable canning factory, required a large redefinition of the firm's purpose, market and product mix before a new dynamic equilibrium was obtained.

Emery and Trist maintain that enterprises like the food canner are designing their organization structures to be appropriate to simpler environments rather than the complex turbulent ones which they are actually facing. A new *design principle* is now required. Organizations by their very nature require what is known in systems theory and information theory as 'redundancy'. By this is meant duplication, replaceability, interchangeability, and these resources are needed to reduce error in the face of variability and change. The traditional technocratic bureaucracy is based on *redundancy of parts*. The parts are broken down so that the ultimate elements are as simple as possible; thus an unskilled worker in a narrow job who is cheap to replace and who takes little time to train would be regarded as an ideal job design. But this approach also requires reliable control systems – often cumbersome and costly.

An alternative design, based on the *redundancy of functions*, is appropriate to turbulent environments. In this approach individuals and units have wide repertoires of activities to cope with change and they are self-regulating. For the individual they create roles rather than mere jobs; for the organization, they bring into being a *variety-increasing* system rather than the traditional control by variety reduction. For this approach to be achieved there has to be continuing development of appropriate new values concerned with improving the *quality of working life* by keeping the technological determinants of worker behaviour to a minimum in order to satisfy social and psychological needs by the involvement of all involved. Autonomous working groups, collaboration rather than competition (between organizations as well as within them) and reduction of hierarchical emphasis, are some of the requirements for operating effectively in modern turbulence. The table opposite sets out the key features of the old and new approaches.

The socio-technical systems approach to jointly achieving effective functioning in a turbulent environment, and to increasing the quality of working life, has also been undertaken at a wider 'macro-social' level.

Features of Old and New Approaches

Old Approach	*New Approach*
The technological imperative	Joint optimization
People as extensions of machines	People as complementary to machines
People as expendable spare parts	People as a resource to be developed
Maximum task breakdown, simple narrow skills	Optimum task grouping, multiple broad skills
External controls (supervisors, specialist staffs, procedures)	Internal controls (self-regulating sub-systems)
Tall organization chart, autocratic style	Flat organization chart, participative style
Competition, gamesmanship	Collaboration, collegiality
Organization's purposes only	Members' and society's purposes also
Alienation	Commitment
Low risk-taking	Innovation

from Trist (1981)

For example, working with the Norwegian social psychologists E. Thorsrud and P. G. Herbst, the Tavistock group have studied the Norwegian shipping industry.

Many technological designs are available for sophisticated bulk carriers. The one chosen was that which best met the social and psychological needs of the small shipboard community that had to live together in isolated conditions, twenty-four hours a day for considerable periods, while efficiently achieving the work tasks. A common mess and a recreation room were established; deck and engine-room crews were integrated, status differences between officers and men were reduced and even eliminated through the development of open career lines and the establishment of 'all officer' ships. Also training for future jobs onshore could be begun at sea.

Without these improvements in the quality of working life, not enough Norwegians would have gone to sea to sustain the Norwegian Merchant Marine which is critical for Norway's economy. Poorly educated and transient foreign crews could not cope with technically sophisticated ships, and alcoholism was dangerously high. These issues could not have been effectively tackled by any one single company; all firms in the industry, several seafaring unions and a number of maritime regulatory organizations all had to be involved in order to sustain the macro-social system development that was required.

The work of Trist and the Tavistock group has been most consistent in applying systems thinking over a large range of sites; the primary work system, the whole organization system and the macro-social domain. In doing so they have illuminated the dynamic nature of organizations and their functioning, the crucial importance of boundary management, and the need for a new approach to organizational design which can accommodate environmental change.

BIBLIOGRAPHY

EMERY, F. E., and TRIST, E. L., 'Socio-technical systems', in C. W. Churchman and M. Verhulst (eds.), *Management Science, Models and Techniques*, vol. 2, Pergamon, 1946; reprinted in F. E. Emery (ed.), *Systems Thinking*, Penguin, 1969.

TRIST, E. L., and BAMFORTH, K. W., 'Some social and psychological consequences of the Longwall method of coal getting', *Human Relations* 4 (1951), 3–38; reprinted in D. S. Pugh (ed.), *Organization Theory*, Penguin, 1990.

TRIST, E. L., *et al.*, *Organizational Choice*, Tavistock, 1963.

EMERY, F. E., and TRIST, E. L., 'The causal texture of organizational environments', *Human Relations* 18 (1965), 21–32; reprinted in F. E. Emery (ed.), *Systems Thinking*, Penguin, 1969.

TRIST, E. L., 'The Socio-technical Perspective', in A. van de Ven and W. F. Joyce (eds.), *Perspectives on Organization Design and Behaviour*, Wiley-Interscience, 1981.

RICE, A. K., *Productivity and Social Organization*, Tavistock, 1958.

EMERY, F. E., and THORSRUD, E., *Democracy at Work*, Martinus Nijhoft (Leiden), 1976.

HERBST, P. G., *Alternatives to Hierarchies*, Martinus Nijhoft (Leiden), 1976.

David Silverman

David Silverman is Reader in Sociology at Goldsmiths' College, University of London. After studying at the London School of Economics, he spent a period in the US before going to his present post. Silverman works within the discipline of sociology and his interest has been to develop a sociological critique of organization theory. Much of his research work has been carried out in public sector organizations, including local government administration and the British National Health Service. He has particularly studied selection processes, administrative occupations and professional–client relationships.

Silverman's main contribution has been the introduction of an 'action-oriented' perspective to organization theory. He has argued that an alternative is needed to what he regards as the dominant perspective in the study of organizations, namely, systems theory. The alternative is to view organizations as the product of the actions and interactions of motivated people pursuing purposes of their own. For Silverman most organizational analysis has been based on a mistaken set of assumptions, the basic mistake being to conceptualize organizations as systems which can be described and understood without reference to the motivations and interpretations of the people in them. Most organization theory involves *reification*, that is, attributing thought and action to social constructs.

Organizational analysis started as a separate area of study, Silverman maintains, by trying to offer answers to questions posed by those who control the operation of organizations, namely, the managers. This has led to a consistent bias through which the analysis of organizations is presented in a dehumanized, neutral way while in fact it is the concerns of managers that are dealt with. This bias is apparent in all established approaches and it is Silverman's purpose to expose such biases and to set up a more satisfactory theory.

By contrast, Silverman distinguishes three characteristics of a formal organization. The first is that it arises at a discernible point in time and is easier than most sets of social relationships to perceive as an artefact. The second is that relationships are taken less for granted by those organizational members who seek to coordinate and control. The third characteristic is that planned changes in social relations and the rules of the game are open to discussion. Thus this definition looks at organizations from the point of view of the social relationships within them and how organizational 'actors' (i.e. the members) interpret and understand them. Silverman's criticisms of organization theory are based on this view.

The dominant theoretical view of organizations sees them as systems and is concerned with general patterns and points of similarity between all organizations, rather than with individual action. A systems view sees organizations as a set of interdependent parts with needs for survival. In adapting to these needs organizations are seen as behaving and taking action. Organizations have to transform a variety of inputs (people, money, materials) into outputs and the process of regulation through which this occurs has been a predominant area of study. But systems theorists fail to consider that it is the *members* of organizations, interpreting what they understand as the environment, importing meanings and common definitions, who do the regulating and adapting.

Because, like so much organizational analysis, systems theory starts from the viewpoint of the executive, it confuses the actions of managers with the behaviour of the organization. In carrying out this abstraction, systems theory directs attention away from purposive human action. Such an approach sees structures as *transcendental*, that is, with a logic of their own and analysable independently of human actions, perceptions and meanings. Silverman sees structures as *immanent*, that is, continuously constructed and reconstructed out of the meanings that actors take from them and give to them. These differences in approach are at the heart of conceptualizing organizations. Given these theoretical structures, the same problems are to be found in the two main variants of systems theory: *functionalism* which is derived from sociology and *socio-technical systems* theory which is inter-disciplinary in character. They are both concerned with the consequences rather than the causes of behaviour. They both rest on a biological analogy which is unsatisfactory for the description and explanation of human events. They both stress processes of adaptation and states of equilibrium and cannot adequately deal with change and conflict. They both involve reification rather than dealing with the sources of orientations of organizational members.

However, within these rather severe limitations, Silverman does see some limited steps forward in the socio-technical systems perspective. The idea of behaviour and motivations as an outcome of technology has involved some writers in dealing with conflicts of interests and strategies. Seeing organizations as interrelations of technology, environment, sentiments and structures, with no one factor dominant, means stressing the absence of any one most efficient form of organization. But in the end any form of systems approach is unable to explain why particular organizations occur; it can only describe patterns of adaptation and their consequences in its own terms.

Silverman also sees problems with the other main approach that he identifies, *organizational psychology*. There is not here the issue of reification and there is a concern with people. But, as with systems theory, the emphasis is still on needs; almost, people as systems. Individuals are conceptualized as having needs to fulfil (e.g. physiological, social, self-actualizing) which form a hierarchy and are often in conflict with organizational goals. Silverman suggests that there are major problems in validating the existence of such needs and that it is not clear whether they would explain behaviour anyway. Also, writers in this approach are far too concerned with general patterns of need and behaviour rather than individual action which, for Silverman, should be at the heart of organizational analysis.

To deal with all the problems inherent in established ways of theorizing about organizations there is only one solution, the adoption of an *action frame of reference*. The essential element in this approach is to view organizations as the outcome of the interaction of motivated people who are attempting to resolve their own problems and pursue their own ends. The environment is conceptualized as a source of meanings for organizational members, being made up of other actors who are defining situations in ways which allow actors inside organizations to defend their own actions and make sense of the actions of others. Some are given significance, others are not. Actions have no meaning other than those given to them by actors.

This method of analysis and theoretical approach is illustrated and developed in the work that Silverman has carried out with Jill Jones on staff-selection interviews in public sector organizations. In empirical terms the emphasis on action, social construction of reality and the development of shared orientations leads to an emphasis on the study of language. It is through language that actions, perceptions and meanings of organizational rules, for example, are established and continuously reaffirmed.

Selection is thus not an objective process of getting the right candidate for the job, but a case of making sense of what goes on in a socially organized setting. In an interview situation, the actors may start with conflicting views of reality or the facts. An outcome has to be managed through verbal exchanges to arrive at an acceptable 'account' of the character of the interviewee and the process of selection. In doing this the actors usually confirm the existing structures of power and authority, shared meanings and rules of operation. The selection process is important in confirming the actors' understanding of what happens and why in the particular organizations of which they are members.

In further studies Silverman compared the specialist–patient interaction in private and National Health Service clinics. In NHS clinics the patient is allocated to a team of doctors, and could well see different ones in successive consultations. The relationship is inevitably largely seen as impersonal. Private patients, by contrast, can organize their relationship to obtain a personalized service since they are perceived by the doctors as being entitled to act like the clients of any fee-paying service. They participate more in the consultation, including asking questions about the experience and competence of the practitioner. They are entitled to evaluate and comment on the service, and they may shop around.

What happens in organizations, then, is a continuous product of motivated human action. For Silverman this is merely emphasizing a general principle of all social life. Because of this it is difficult to distinguish organizations as entities from other types of social structures – and not worth it. The study of organizations should not be seen as an end in itself but as a setting within which general social processes can be studied from a clear *sociological* perspective. By doing this it is possible to ensure that analysts do not impose their own or management's view of what the issues and problems are.

BIBLIOGRAPHY

SILVERMAN, D., *The Theory of Organizations*, Heinemann, 1970.

SILVERMAN, D., and JONES, J., *Organizational Work: The Language of Grading: The Grading of Language*, Collier Macmillan, 1976.

SILVERMAN, D., 'Going Private', *Sociology*, 18, (1984), 191–204; reprinted in D. S. Pugh (ed.), *Organization Theory*, Penguin, 1990.

Name Index

Subject Index

PENGUIN BUSINESS AND ECONOMICS

Almost Everyone's Guide to Economics J. K. Galbraith and Nicole Salinger

This instructive and entertaining dialogue provides a step-by-step explanation of 'the state of economics in general and the reasons for its present failure in particular in simple, accurate language that everyone could understand and that a perverse few might conceivably enjoy'.

The Rise and Fall of Monetarism David Smith

Now that even Conservatives have consigned monetarism to the scrap-heap of history, David Smith draws out the unhappy lessons of a fundamentally flawed economic experiments, driven by a doctrine that for years had been regarded as outmoded and irrelevant.

Atlas of Management Thinking Edward de Bono

This fascinating book provides a vital repertoire of non-verbal images that will help activate the right side of any manager's brain.

The Economists Economics Rupert Pennant-Rea and Clive Crook

Based on a series of 'briefs' published in *The Economist*, this is a clear and accessible guide to the key issues of today's economics for the general reader.

Parkinson's Law C. Northcote Parkinson

'Work expands so as to fill the time available for its completion': that law underlies this 'extraordinarily funny and witty book' (Stephen Potter in the *Sunday Times*) which also makes some painfully serious points about those in business or the Civil Service.

The Winning Streak Walter Goldsmith and David Clutterbuck

A brilliant analysis of what Britain's best-run and most successful companies have in common – a must for all managers.

PENGUIN PHILOSOPHY

I: The Philosophy and Psychology of Personal Identity **Jonathan Glover**

From cases of split brains and multiple personalities to the importance of memory and recognition by others, the author of *Causing Death and Saving Lives* tackles the vexed questions of personal identity. 'Fascinating . . . the ideas which Glover pours forth in profusion deserve more detailed consideration' – Anthony Storr

Minds, Brains and Science **John Searle**

Based on Professor Searle's acclaimed series of Reith Lectures, *Minds, Brains and Science* is 'punchy and engaging . . . a timely exposé of those woolly-minded computer-lovers who believe that computers can think, and indeed that the human mind is just a biological computer' – *The Times Literary Supplement*

Ethics **Inventing Right and Wrong** **J. L. Mackie**

Widely used as a text, Mackie's complete and clear treatise on moral theory deals with the status and content of ethics, sketches a practical moral system and examines the frontiers at which ethics touches psychology, theology, law and politics.

The Penguin History of Western Philosophy **D. W. Hamlyn**

'Well-crafted and readable . . . neither laden with footnotes nor weighed down with technical language . . . a general guide to three millennia of philosophizing in the West' – *The Times Literary Supplement*

Science and Philosophy: Past and Present **Derek Gjertsen**

Philosophy and science, once intimately connected, are today often seen as widely different disciplines. Ranging from Aristotle to Einstein, from quantum theory to renaissance magic, Confucius and parapsychology, this penetrating and original study shows such a view to be both naive and ill-informed.

The Problem of Knowledge **A. J. Ayer**

How do you *know* that is a book? How do you *know* that you know? In *The Problem of Knowledge* A. J. Ayer presented the sceptic's arguments as forcefully as possible, investigating the extent to which they can be met. 'Thorough . . . penetrating, vigorous . . . readable and manageable' – *Spectator*

PENGUIN POLITICS AND SOCIAL SCIENCES

Political Ideas David Thomson (ed.)

From Machiavelli to Marx – a stimulating and informative introduction to the last 500 years of European political thinkers and political thought.

Karl Marx: Selected Writings in Sociology and Social Philosophy
T. B. Bottomore and Maximilien Rubel (eds.)

'It makes available, in coherent form and lucid English, some of Marx's most important ideas. As an introduction to Marx's thought, it has very few rivals indeed' – *British Journal of Sociology*

Post-War Britain A Political History Alan Sked and Chris Cook

Major political figures from Attlee to Thatcher, the aims and achievements of governments and the changing fortunes of Britain in the period since 1945 are thoroughly scrutinized in this stimulating history.

Inside the Third World Paul Harrison

From climate and colonialism to land hunger, exploding cities and illiteracy, this comprehensive book brings home a wealth of facts and analysis on the often tragic realities of life for the poor people and communities of Asia, Africa and Latin America.

Housewife Ann Oakley

'A fresh and challenging account' – *Economist*. 'Informative and rational enough to deserve a serious place in any discussion on the position of women in modern society' – *The Times Educational Supplement*

The Raw and the Cooked Claude Lévi-Strauss

Deliberately, brilliantly and inimatably challenging, Lévi-Strauss's seminal work of structural anthropology cuts wide and deep into the mind of mankind, as he finds in the myths of the South American Indians a comprehensible psychological pattern.

PENGUIN POLITICS AND SOCIAL SCIENCES

Comparative Government S. E. Finer

'A considerable *tour de force* . . . few teachers of politics in Britain would fail to learn a great deal from it . . . Above all, it is the work of a great teacher who breathes into every page his own enthusiasm for the discipline' – Anthony King in *New Society*

On Revolution Hannah Arendt

Arendt's classic analysis of a relatively recent political phenomenon examines the underlying principles common to all revolutions, and the evolution of revolutionary theory and practice. 'Never dull, enormously erudite, always imaginative' – *Sunday Times*

The Apartheid Handbook Roger Omond

The facts behind the headlines: the essential hard information about how apartheid actually works from day to day.

The Social Construction of Reality Peter Berger and Thomas Luckmann

Concerned with the sociology of 'everything that passes for knowledge in society' and particularly with that which passes for common sense, this is 'a serious, open-minded book, upon a serious subject' – *Listener*

The Care of the Self Michel Foucault
The History of Sexuality Vol 3

Foucault examines the transformation of sexual discourse from the Hellenistic to the Roman world in an inquiry which 'bristles with provocative insights into the tangled liaison of sex and self' – *The Times Higher Educational Supplement*

How the Other Half Dies The Real Reasons for World Hunger Susan George

With solid evidence and with conviction, Susan George demonstrates that the fundamental cause of world hunger is the control of food by the world's rich. Only those fortunate people who can become consumers will eat in the Brave New World being shaped by the well-fed.

PENGUIN HISTORY

The Victorian Underworld Kellow Chesney

A superbly evocative survey of the vast substratum of vice that lay below the respectable surface of Victorian England – the showmen, religious fakes, garrotters, pickpockets and prostitutes – and of the penal methods of that 'most enlightened age'. 'Charged with nightmare detail' – *Sunday Times*

A History of Modern France Alfred Cobban

Professor Cobban's renowned three-volume history, skilfully steering the reader through France's political and social problems from 1715 to the Third Republic, remains essential reading for anyone wishing to understand the development of a great European nation.

Stalin Isaac Deutscher

'The Greatest Genius in History' and the 'Life-Giving Force of Socialism'? Or a tyrant more ruthless than Ivan the Terrible and a revolutionary whose policies facilitated the rise of Nazism? An outstanding biographical study of a revolutionary despot by a great historian.

A History of Christianity Paul Johnson

'Masterly ... It is a huge and crowded canvas – a tremendous theme running through twenty centuries of history – a cosmic soap opera involving kings and beggars, philosophers and crackpots, scholars and illiterate *exaltés*, popes and pilgrims and wild anchorites in the wilderness' – Malcolm Muggeridge

The Habsburg Monarch 1809–1918 A. J. P. Taylor

Dissolved in 1918, the Habsburg Empire 'had a unique character, out of time and out of place'. Scholarly and vividly accessible, this 'very good book indeed' (*Spectator*) elucidates the problems always inherent in the attempt to give peace, stability and a common loyalty to a heterogeneous population.

Industry and Empire E. J. Hobsbawm

Volume 3 of the *Penguin Economic History of Britain* covers the period of the Industrial Revolution: 'the most fundamental transformation in the history of the world recorded in written documents.' 'A book that attracts and deserves attention ... by far the most gifted historian now writing' – John Vaizey in the *Listener*

PENGUIN HISTORY

The Penguin History of the United States Hugh Brogan

'An extraordinarily engaging book' – *The Times Literary Supplement*. 'Compelling reading ... Hugh Brogan's book will delight the general reader as much as the student' – *The Times Educational Supplement*. 'He will be welcomed by American readers no less than those in his own country' – J. K. Galbraith

The Making of the English Working Class E. P. Thompson

Probably the most imaginative – and the most famous – post-war work of English social history.

The Waning of the Middle Ages Johan Huizinga

A magnificent study of life, thought and art in 14th- and 15th-century France and the Netherlands, long established as a classic.

The City in History Lewis Mumford

Often prophetic in tone and containing a wealth of photographs, *The City in History* is among the most deeply learned and warmly human studies of man as a social creature.

The Second World War A. J. P. Taylor

A brilliant and detailed illustrated history, enlivened by all Professor Taylor's customary iconaclasm and it.

Inside Nazi Germany Conformity, Opposition and Racism in Everyday Life
Detlev J. K. Peukert

An authoritative study – and a challenging and original analysis – of the realities of daily existence under the Third Reich. 'A fascinating study ... captures the whole range of popular attitudes and the complexity of their relationship with the Nazi state' – Richard Geary